# Northern Stars

## A story of God's unfailing love

Anna Legaspi

authorHOUSE®

AuthorHouse™ LLC
1663 Liberty Drive
Bloomington, IN 47403
www.authorhouse.com
Phone: 1-800-839-8640

Published by AuthorHouse  01/15/2014

ISBN: 978-1-4918-4536-3 (sc)
ISBN: 978-1-4918-4535-6 (e)

Library of Congress Control Number:  2013923083

# Acknowledgements

Although the names of individuals have been changed to protect their true identity, if you had been part of Anna's journey, you will know without a doubt if you were one of the characters.

Anna's journey included incidences of provision, lack, testing and suffering, astonishment, disbelief, mercy, anger and deliverance.

Anna is deeply grateful to any and everyone that God has used. Writing the book began with the intention of relating how Anna would eventually find the man who truly loves her. Little did she know that fate would change the final chapter of her book to lead her back in the arms of the one who loved her from the very beginning.

To God be the glory forever Amen.

# Northern Stars

". . . every long lost dream led me to where you are. Others who broke my heart, they were just Northern stars—pointing me on my way into your loving arms . . . that God blessed the broken road that led me straight to you . . . ."

(lyrics from "God bless the Broken Road" song By Rascal Flatts)

# Contents

# Chapter 1

## Anna

Anna, as her parents called her, was born in a poor family from a 3$^{rd}$ world country—Philippines. But even a poor family in the Philippines can have a maid . . . a direct reflection of how cheap labor was in that country.

Her parents only had two kids. Anna was the older child and was expected to give and be more tolerant to her younger sibling Dong (a nickname given to her sister by her dad who wanted a boy instead of another girl). If Anna wanted something and her younger sister Dong wanted it as well, she was always told by her parents to let her younger sister have it. She was after all, "the" big sister.

Anna was raised catholic. From it was instilled the fear of God—extending from, but not limited to, the responsibility of always giving being that she is the older sibling. From clothes, shoes, friends, schools, Anna always gave to what her sister wanted.

### Dong's Braces

In college, her sister Dong wanted braces for her teeth because it was a status symbol. Only rich kids can afford a dentist, much less have braces. Dong got it! Anna was coerced by her mom to agree to share the dental expenses to give Dong what she wanted. Dong was her mom's favorite child . . . something Anna could not understand. She always thought parents can't have favorites since it was their decision to bring forth the children in the first place.

Anna worked three jobs after graduating from college to earn the money to pay for her sister's braces. She worked as a full time occupational therapist, a grade school home tutor and a home health therapist on the weekends. Being a therapist was a respectable profession in her country. She made about 25 pesos or what is now equal to about 50 cents an hour in the US. Her weekend home health job paid better and yielded a whopping 200 pesos or approximately $4/visit.

Anna always had it in her heart to want to give her parents and family a better life—food, money, clothing, access to nice places and restaurants, but more importantly, the ability to give money or aid to total strangers.

## Late Bloomer

Anna grew up Ms. Goody-goody two shoes. Her sister who was only a year younger use to laugh at her for the comments and questions she would ask her younger sister whenever she told Anna of her shenanigans with boys. One day, Dong came home from school and motioned Anna to follow her to the bedroom. Quickly shutting the door behind after Anna got in the room, Dong excitedly disclosed to Anna her first kissing experience with a boy from her class.

"Anna, I had my first lips to lips today!" Dong giggled.

"How was it?" Anna asked. Anna was already in first year college and her sister still in high school.

"It was great!" Dong blurted.

Growing up raised Catholics by strict parents was never going to let Dong keep her from doing what she wanted when she wanted.

Having never been kissed, Anna inquired with all innocence.

"How do you guys do it? Do you have to first discuss between the two of you who gets the top lip or the bottom lip? How do you know when to breathe?" she badgered.

"You will just know," Dong responded as she sighed in frustration.

"Oh my God, you are such a prude! You are the older one and I have to teach you these things?" Dong continued.

## Hickies

Dong's response triggered another memory flash back in Anna's thoughts. They were a lot younger back then. Anna was 10 and Dong was 9 years old. Anna was down in the living room watching TV when she heard a loud sound followed by Dong's loud squeal.

What came afterward was the sound of Dong's footsteps as she ran down from their parent's bedroom sobbing.

"What happened?" Anna probed.

"Mom saw the marks on my arm," Dong explained as she pointed to the culpable marks.

"What are those?" Anna asked as her naiveté kept her from recognizing the mark.

Still sobbing, Dong began expounding, "I was watching some people kissing on TV and I tried to practice on my arms and it left these marks."

"Do they hurt?" Anna questioned.

"Not really."

"The wooden ruler she hit me with on my butt when she saw them hurt more." Dong commented.

It wasn't until hours later that Anna would realize, after listening in on her mom reporting to her dad what happened, that the marks were Dong's self-inflicted "hickies."

Anna's wandering thoughts were brought back to the present by the sound of their mom yelling, "Food is ready."

## Admission

"What is occupational therapy?" she remembered asking herself with a wrinkled nose when she first saw her name under the roster of students admitted to the university where she applied. Students were admitted to the program of their choice based on their admissions' test ranking score. Applicants to that university were mostly honor students from different high schools—public and private. Only the first top scoring 40 students who picked physical therapy as their first choice, were admitted to the program. Then the next top 40 students get admitted to the program of their second choice. She remembers every classmate wanting to be in physical therapy for the prospect of going to the U.S. as there was a shortage of therapists in that country at that time. She herself, applied for physical therapy as her first choice. At the said university where she applied, almost every student is of high IQs. Only the rich and/or the extremely poor, but intelligent kid, get admitted. Some are children of politicians or business owners and others are children of poverty.

## The DREAM

In that university, each student's tuition is based on family income. As such, children from higher income paid higher tuition fees than those who are impoverished. Anna was one such student. Her whole 4-year B.S. college degree only cost what would be equivalent to less than $1000 USD. She only had to pay for books each semester. Her parents were categorized as being from a very low income family. The only thing she had to do is maintain good grades. So she did.

When she finally graduated, Anna prepared to take the board exam. It was necessary before she could practice her chosen profession. She couldn't afford the American books that all her other rich classmates had like "Willard and Spackman", "Pedretti" and "Trombly" so she relied mainly on her notes from lectures as she prepared for the dreaded exam. She took shorthand classes back in high school which helped her take down quick and fairly accurate lecture notes. She asked to borrow her classmates' books but since everyone else was also preparing for the exam, no one wanted to part with their books.

Luckily, a day before the board exam, one classmate named Eugene did agree to let her borrow one of his books. She was thrilled and very thankful.

Once she had the book on her hands, she realized that the book had over 400 hundred pages at least. Now she has another problem . . . where to even begin.

Growing up being timid made her have very few friends and as such, she often resorted to talking to God. She said out loud while looking up, "Oh Lord, now we got a problem. Do you see how many pages there are in this book? There is no way I can read and memorize all of these a few hours before the board. I also have to sleep you know?"

She demanded out loud. " You have to tell me what chapters to read—only those which will be included in the test. I can't read all of these pages. You ready?"

Anna closed her eyes and just followed whatever popped in her head. She did not follow the chapters in the book or went in any particular order. Whatever popped in her mind is what she read. She fell asleep studying and the next day took the test.

Days before the results of the exam was to be revealed, Anna had a dream. She dreamt of the number "4". It was in color and the story didn't make sense—just the number "4" in color. She was working at the pediatric hospital at the time and had a friend named Beth who is a born again Christian.

"You know Beth, I had a weird dream last night, something about the number 4," Anna shared.

"We didn't talk about anything pertaining to number 4. I didn't read or watch anything about the number four so I don't know why it would appear so vividly in my dream?", she inquired. "You know what it means?" she continued.

"I have no earthly idea." Beth replied as she quickly changed the subject.

"You know the board exam results come out today. Want to come with me after work to find out later if we passed?" Beth asked.

They were both on temporary licenses awaiting exam results.

"OK." Anna responded even though she was still preoccupied about her dream.

Later that day they found themselves at the office where all test results for any kind of nationwide certification or licensure is released. Beth had found the roster of board passers for occupational therapy. Anna nervously looked and scrolled at the posted roster and found her name. "

"Oh thank God!" she muttered as she realized she passed the exam. That was all she wanted anyway.

"Anna, look!" Beth exclaimed in amazement.

"What?" Anna responded.

Beth's index finger pointed at the number before Anna's name . . . . the number "4". Anna ranked Top 4 in the whole country, not just for her school, for that year's nationwide board exam.

"Your dream!" Beth continued.

Anna was speechless. She could not believe it. She knows there are other classmates with far better resources and more studying time than she ever had. She remembers complaining to herself about how she has to wash the family's weekly clothes every Saturday and then iron all of them every Sunday. She envied how her rich classmates have all the time to study. Time she didn't have. She was stunned. Deep down, Anna wondered . . . was it God, or was it just chance? She didn't have the answer.

# Chapter 2

## Coming to America

Anna started getting offers to come to the U.S to work while she was still only on her $3^{rd}$ year in college. She told the recruiters to call her back when she graduated and amazingly they did.

Anna noticed how a lot of the therapists she knew, had already flown and accepted jobs in the U.S. Now the country is left with younger, less-experienced therapists. She decided to stay and be a clinical instructor to help combat what was termed "brain-drain" (with therapists leaving abroad to earn a greater financial pay). Anna completed her degree accordingly. She knew she had to. Her parents were relying on her to help improve the family's financial situation. Surprisingly enough, one persistent recruiter from the US called her again a year after and asked her, "Are you ready to come to the US now?" her name was Kathy or was it? She couldn't remember.

Anna's batch mates were also getting offers to come to U.S to work. Although she has never been away from her family and grew up extremely timid, the prospect of earning $35,000/year is something that would take her at least 10 years to make if she opted to stay in the Philippines. Thirty five thousand dollars would be close to 1,500,000 pesos depending on the exchange rate—an amount she could not even comprehend then.

Unsure of what to do, Anna decided to lock herself in the bedroom to pray.

## The Conversion

"Sssshhhh . . . . be quiet!" she remembers her mother telling her and sister as the evangelicals/ protestants knock on their door. Anna's country is predominantly catholic. About 80% of the population is Catholic and the rest "protestants". That's how her parents referred to anyone who went to any church—Baptist, Pentecostal, Methodist, other than Catholic. But there's only a few percentage of evangelical Christians who regularly knock on people's door, especially during the weekends, to share the "good news."

Her mother always ordered them to never entertain "those" people. Even when it is obvious to those people that someone is inside the house, her mother would strictly instruct them to be quiet and pretend that there is no one in the house until those people left. Something she always found very rude and callous to do. She used to wonder what's the difference between the two, since Catholics considered themselves Christians and so did the protestants.

They go through this at least every other month since "those" people were very dedicated.

One weekend, Anna was by herself in their house.

She heard a knock and peeked at the window. She saw the "dreaded" people.

It always made her wonder what those people have that they want so badly to share with others. She admired the fact that they are willing to endure people being rude to them or walking under the heat of the sun every weekend. "How bad could it be if you let them in?" She asked herself.

Anna found herself opening the door and letting the two individuals in. They were very polite and grateful for the opportunity Anna gave them. They wore what Anna categorized as "church clothes". The man wore a white long sleeve shirt and black slacks while the lady wore a white blouse and black skirt. Her hair was pulled backed in a pony tail. The "plain Jane" look Anna thought.

They sat down after she gestured them to have a seat. They opened their bible and just shared the gist of their religious beliefs with her. They also said that nothing is an accident. They read to her verses from the book of John from the New Testament. She was waiting for the individuals to ask her for money or act crazy since her mother always warned them about these kinds of individuals but nothing happened yet.

Before long, the individuals told her that they were ready to get going but wanted to see if she would join them in prayer to receive Jesus Christ as her Lord and Savior. She didn't see anything wrong with it so she did. They asked her to start reading the bible and find a bible-based church to join or attend. They got up, congratulated her for the wonderful decision of being "born again" and headed out towards the door.

"That's it? That's all you want?" she said in a whisper behind their backs.

## The Promise

Before that day she accepted Christ in her heart, Anna's prayers were mostly memorized words of prayer taught from school. Since her acceptance, she has learned, in reading the bible, to pray as if she was just talking to God. She also read chapters were people found God's favor by humbling and kneeling before God. She needed to make a very important decision. Today she needed to pray. She is receiving offers to come to the US when others had to bribe recruiting agencies and pay them thousands of pesos to help them find jobs abroad.

She got down on her knees, locked herself in one of the bedrooms and began to pray. She asked to be used as a vessel to help others while at the same time allowing her to make money for her family. She remembers saying,

"God, tell me what to do. It said in the Old Testament that you use to talk to prophets and that people could actually hear you. But now, not anymore," she paused. She always saw and referred to herself as baby Christian as she did not know how to pray like how she has heard others pray. Their prayers always seem more "holy-sounding" compared to hers, is what she thought. Yet still, she continued to pray.

"I will close my eyes and close this bible in front of me. When I open it, You will lead my hand to point to the answer to my question, ok?" as if trying to boss God to come to her terms.

She closed her eyes, paused and then opened the bible. Using her right hand index finger she points to a verse with her eyes closed.

"Here we go Lord," she said skeptically.

With her right hand index finger pointed up in the air, eyes closed and knees in prayer, she opened the bible she held in front of her and in her mind said, "Wherever my finger ends up is what Your message is for me."

She opened the bible only with her sense of touch (as her eyes were still closed) and she pointed down her finger on the bible and kept it there. She slowly opened her eyes and proceeded to read where her finger had landed. The word says, " . . . for I know my plans for you—plans to prosper you and not to harm you, plans to give you a future."

"This is ridiculous!!!" she quietly said to herself.

She asked, "Does this mean I should go to the US?" She waited but didn't hear an audible answer. She then made up her mind that THAT was her answer.

"I take it that I am going to the US?" she asked again her ethereal friend—God.

So she did. She accepted the offer to work and came to the US. That verse Jeremiah 29:11 is the first verse she has ever memorized since accepting Christ.

## Airplane with Ling

The recruiter paired Anna with another therapist recruit from a different school—Ling. Unlike Anna, Ling's dad had money. She wanted to come to the US just to be in the US. She did not need to help her parents financially. With only $100 in her pocket, Anna was headed to the U.S.

The airplane ride was a hoot. They both have never been on an airplane. They agreed that they would watch what everyone else is doing and copy. From how to put on their seat belts, how to order their meals, how to adjust the temperature, how to call for a flight attendant etc, copy they did. They laughed and giggled at every mistake they did, but it was all fun, they were, after all, coming to the US.

The plane landed on time and they were greeted by an Indian—looking gentleman. He said his name is Matt and introduced himself as the "right-hand" of the owner of the company who hired them. He drove them from the airport to their motels. They were there for at least 2 weeks while the said gentleman tried to get them an apartment and helped them get all the necessary documentation—social security cards, professional license, driver's license, etc.

## Operator

During their first night in the US, Ling tried to use the phone to make an international call to her family to let them know she arrived in the US safely.

"Hello?" Anna heard Ling say.

Then all of a sudden Ling frantically gestured Anna to take the phone from her.

"I can't understand what she is saying," Ling told Anna in a whisper as she covered the phone's mouthpiece with both hands.

"Hello?" Anna answered as she took the phone from Ling.

"Operator, How may I assist you?" Anna heard.

"Oooohhh . . . operator!" Anna exclaimed in relief of the fact that she understood what the lady on the other end of the line was saying.

Anna quickly hung up in panic as she was unsure how much they will be charged the longer they stayed on the phone with the operator.

"She said op-ray-ter." Anna told Ling.

"The Americans don't seem to pronounce every other syllable like we do," Anna continued. The lady seemed to pronounce "or" as "er", Anna thought.

"Remember how we heard someone say "fity" instead of fifty? Just talk lazy and we can understand them better," Anna added as if she had it all figured out.

"Whew! Sorry I panicked. I thought she said "upper right hand corner" and I did not know what to say," Ling replied.

They both laughed at their first "lost-in-translation"-like experience and began unpacking their bags.

Seeing that where they were, was not the US they had seen on TV (as most of the American TV shows they watched showed New York or California), they began to wonder if they were really in the US. They feared that they had been duped and might have to be factory workers for the rest of their lives never see their families again.

Such was not the case. They soon moved into an apartment and began working in the respective facilities where they were assigned. In a few months, they both passed the US therapy licensure exam and started learning more about the Americans. The recruiter who helped Anna gave her the book, "How to Survive In The US," as a souvenir. The book explained and provided 1)pictures of US currency— cent, nickel , dime, quarter, etc, 2) possible scenarios when they might interact with Americans 3) usual forms of greeting and how to respond accordingly to terms such as "Howdy?"

## Sauce

The next day, Anna and Ling woke up and decided to venture and find somewhere to eat. The motel were they stayed was in a somewhat busy intersection. They saw something very familiar to them—the yellow "M" of McDonalds. They went in enthusiastically.

Anna went by the counter and ordered coffee.

"What sauce?" the employee standing behind the counter inquired.

Anna was confused.

"They serve coffee with sauce here?" is what she asked herself. In her country, they only add cream and/or sugar to their coffee.

Anna remembered the survival book saying something about observing others and pretending to know. It was a chapter on fake it 'til you make it" kind of thing.

Anna responded back with a question, "Well what do you have?"

The employee rolled her eyes as if telling Anna "duh" and said, " . . . small . . . medium . . . large."

"Ohhhh . . . . what size!" Anna exclaimed with a smile of relief on her face.

It was another learning experience for Anna with regards to the "southerners".


## The Billfold


Anna was always grateful for the opportunity of coming to the US. She made it her goal to try and learn something everyday.

One day at work, a patient asked Anna to do something.

"Anna, can you look for my billfold? I have a doctor's appointment," Mr. G requested.

"Sure sir. Let me look for it." Anna politely answered.

Anna started opening the top drawer. She saw grooming supplies.

"Hmmnnn . . . not there," Anna told herself.

She went through the next drawer, then the next one and again said, "Nope. It's not there."

She opened the bottom drawer, saw a wallet and a couple pieces of paper, closed the drawer back and said, "Not there either."

Anna searched the closet by the door which took another five minutes. She looked under the bed, by the window sill, behind the TV, and even checked the bathroom.

Perturbed, Anna disappointedly told Mr.G, "I am so sorry sir. I couldn't find your billfold. I searched everywhere. I even checked the bathroom."

Mr.G replied, "Oh no. I really need it."

He asked if she could open each drawer again and take out what was inside and show it to him as he couldn't see them while he was lying in bed.

Anna obliged. She went and re-opened the top drawer, lifted and showed each item to Mr. G. She then returned items back after Mr. G motioned her to do so. She repeated the same action as she went through each drawer.

"He is keeping me up. I need to be with my next patient," she quietly reminded herself in case she forgot.

She opened the bottom drawer and without saying a word, showed Mr. G the brown leather wallet and the papers.

"That's it!" Mr. G yelled in relief as he pointed to the wallet.

"This? This is a wallet," she told Mr. G in case he could not see well and did not know what a wallet looked like.

"I know! That is a wallet," the elderly agreed.

"All along I have been looking for a dollar bill that was folded," Anna explained as she shook her head in embarrassment as she realized she was looking for the wrong thing all along.

Mr. G laughed and said, "Yes Anna. A wallet is the same as a billfold."

Anna and Ling were both very competitive and fast learners. On the weekends, they started driving to other cities to continue to learn more. They started dating and soon started having separate lives. Anna went on to date the individual who received them at the airport during their arrival, while Ling ended up dating an accountant.

## The "pay error"

Anna started working. Every month, she kept a third of her net pay and sent the other two thirds to her family. She slept in a sleeping bag and only had a radio in her apartment to let her know how the weather was the next day so she could dress appropriately for work.

After about six months of being in the US, her mother phoned her to tell her that they (her parents) were being evicted. Anna's mother was asking her to send more money than she had already been doing. She didn't know what else to do. She was already sending more than half of her net pay and didn't know of any other way to produce money.

She remembers, back when she was still in her country, that she had seen some TV program of church people making testimonies of different "miracles" God had done for them. Those who gave testimonies were in tears and couldn't speak enough of the goodness of God.

She still considered herself as a "baby Christian" and liked putting her learning to test.

She decided to pray.

Anna commenced, "Lord, I have seen others with tears of joy speaking of Your mercy and grace. I want to experience it."

She explained to God her parents' money situation, as if God didn't know. She even reminded God that it said in the bible that, "ask and you shall receive, seek and you shall find, knock and it shall be opened . . ."

She continued, "Lord I am asking, I am seeking, I am knocking. Do something about this situation." She ended her prayer with the words "In Jesus' name" and decided to not at all worry about it.

The next paycheck she received was over by $500 than what she was supposed to receive after all taxes and health insurance had been taken out.

"This is a mistake," she thought. She then worried that she was getting someone else's pay as she knew of another Anna who has been with the company for about five years. She picked up the phone and called to speak with someone from the payroll department. She explained the "mistake" and asked them to please correct the issue immediately so she will not be tempted to spend the money. The payroll person on the other line asked her questions to verify her information prior to checking on the matter and asked if she could place her on hold.

"Ma'am, I am so sorry for the wait but our records indicate that, THAT, is what you are supposed to receive," the payroll personnel said.

"Oh no, no,no," Anna said in disappointment.

"I'm sorry but you are clearly mistaken," she insisted.

"I have only been in this country for six months and I even have my contract with me to prove it," she stated calmly.

"Would you like me to fax you a copy of my contract?" she added, to which the personnel declined.

She told Anna that she would direct her concern to someone higher up as there was nothing else she could do at the moment.

Anna pleaded with the lady to please do so and have someone get back to her immediately as possible as she didn't want the same error on her next paycheck.

The next payday came and just as she had feared, it was again over $500. She called the payroll department again and requested for someone "higher up". She went through the same verification questioning only to be told the same thing . . . .

"Ma'am our records indicate that is what you should be getting," the personnel stated.

Anna was very frustrated. She again offered to send a copy of her contract as proof of what she should only be getting. The personnel declined insisting that what was showing up on her screen was the correct information. Anna flustered at the error, tried to compose herself and courteously requested to escalate and direct her issue to someone higher up.

Another pay day came and still the same error. Anna was finally able to get on the phone with whoever was highest in that company's payroll department. She goes through the same verification-of—identity questioning and was placed on hold yet again.

"I'm sorry ma'am but our records show that you are receiving what you are supposed to get," the payroll department manager stated.

"You don't understand. I have tried to speak with several people from your department to correct the issue and for weeks now, still nothing has been done," complained Anna.

"I'm sorry Anna but this is what we have. We have plenty of people complaining that they were getting less than they should. You are actually the only person getting more than what you say you should but our records show that THAT is what you should be getting. Maybe when you start getting less you could call us back. I don't know what else I could do for you," the manager countered sarcastically.

"I'm sorry I could not be of further help. Goodbye." The manager said as she hung up.

Anna was at a loss for words. Then she had her "aha' moment and said as she looked up at the ceiling, "is this the answer to what I've asked?" She smiled and sent the extra money to her family to keep them from getting evicted.

Anna's "payroll error" continued for the next six to eight months until her parents' house has been paid in full.

# Chapter 3

## The First Fall

Anna has never dated much in college. She was too busy helping her family. When she came to the US at age 21, she was ill-prepared with matters of the heart. Americans start dating in their teens. She was way far behind. She didn't have enough experience and wasn't even sure of what she wanted in a man.

Fortunately or unfortunately, Anna's guy proposed after eight months of dating. In the back of her mind, Anna always worried about the fact that they were of different faith. She believed in Christianity and he followed Hinduism.

In an effort to be on her good side, Matt did go to church with her on Sundays. He usually sits beside her antsy and eager for the service to be over as he says to her he could be making money instead of sitting there. She just ignored his comments and thought that over time, he would eventually come to know and appreciate her God.

### Unequally Yoked

While they were still dating, during one of Anna's quiet time with God, a verse came to mind. It was 2 Corinthians 6:14. As she opened her bible to search the verse, she found the verse almost reprimanding her, "Be ye not unequally yoked together with unbelievers . . ." it said. She got somewhat fearful and did not want to continue to read the rest of the verse. She remembered how in certain chapters of the old testament that she has read in the past, people were severely punished for disobeying the Lord. She knew in her heart that she had sinned. She not only fornicated but also with an unbeliever.

He was the first person she had been intimate with. She even remembered the bleeding and the pain when they first did it. She realized that night that she was no longer a virgin. She felt ashamed. In her culture, that was only supposed to happen on the night of one's marriage. She remembered her father saying, "No one would marry you unless you are a virgin." It kept repeating in her head constantly reminding her of how important one's virginity is in their culture.

Though hesitant, she accepted the proposal. It was the only way she knew to save face for her parent's sake. They had two weddings —one in his country and one in hers. They spent a decent amount of money for their weddings as they both made $120,000 yearly together. He, too, worked in an allied medical field.

For three years of marriage, Anna only knew how to drive to work and back to home. She was never allowed by her husband Matt to go anywhere else without him. Although they made almost the same income, Anna's husband handled the finances and only gave her $20 or $40 a week if she asked and explained what it was for. Anna had witnessed growing up how her parents fought about money quite a few times and she had promised herself at an early age that she would not allow money to be an issue in her marriage.

When Anna wanted to send money to her family, the very reason why she came in the US to begin with, she had to tell Matt the exact amount she wants to send and why it was needed. It was almost like applying for a scholarship requiring a great essay of why your deserve it. She didn't see anything wrong with it at the time, as she was raised to believe that a married woman should always listen to her husband.

She later realized that her husband was very controlling and verbally and emotionally abusive. She started feeling that she was not being appreciated and was always compared to his mom. He expected her to work a full time job, hand all her money to him but also do all the wifely duties of cooking, cleaning, doing laundry, ironing clothes etc. Yet she had no say or input whatsoever with any decisions that affected both of them.

During one of their dinner, Anna had cooked immediately after she came home from work.

When Matt came home, the dinner table was already set. The plates, the pitcher and the glass of water, a bowl of rice, and meat casserole from his country with recipe that she looked up on the internet. Anna wanted to surprise him.

Anna was shocked to hear what came out of his mouth as she was expecting to hear positive words thinking the meal she prepared was a labor of love considering she was exhausted from a long day at work.

"Where's the salad?" Matt asked seemingly annoyed.

"What salad?" she countered.

"You are supposed to have a salad before the main dish!" Matt emphasized.

"Huh? I'm sorry. I was not aware of that," Anna quickly apologized.

"Where's the soup?" Matt asked.

"What soup?" Anna replied disconcertingly.

"You are supposed to have a soup to go with every dish!" Matt stressed.

"Uhmmnnn . . . . .I am sorry. I didn't know that either. I will try to do better next time," she promised.

"You better," were the last words Anna heard from Matt before he proceeded eating.

Anna felt unappreciated.

## More unappreciations

Anna learned more about Matt's culture. She noticed how, when they would visit his friends who are also mostly from his country, most of the wives gathered in the kitchen talking about food, household chores and children while the men talked about finances.

When he would have one of his friends visit, he would tell her to sleep in the living room and him and his friend would sleep in the bedroom. Not that they were gay but that in their culture, men seemed more important than women. In an effort to be a good host, Matt would let his friend sleep on the bed while Anna was told to sleep in the living room floor.

During meals, her husband would point to his glass and look at her to indicate that he wants her to fill his glass with water even though the pitcher of water was only less than a foot away from him and all he had to do was extend his arm out.

He was also always very critical of her and did not like it when other people complimented her on anything. He would repeatedly tell her that she is not as good of a driver as he is and not as good of a clinician as he is since he has about nine years experience of being in the US ahead of her.

## The Stock Market

Matt was a very proud man. He studied and learned day trading and made about approximately thirty thousand dollars during his first six months. He even contemplated just doing therapy on the side and being a full time day trader based on how well he had done so far. Unfortunately one day, the stock market crashed. Matt lost about $150,000 of their savings.

He didn't tell Anna right away. After a week, he did eventually, over dinner. He did not apologize for losing her money. Instead of being mad, Anna was very supportive.

"Oh by the way, I lost about $150,000 of our money in the stock market last week," he opened.

"It was not my fault. The market crashed," he ended.

"It's only money," she assured him believing that continuing to be kind to him would eventually change him and not make him so controlling and abusive.

"We are young and we have our health. Everything will be okay." She added.

## The Interpretation

As the months went by however, her "eyes" slowly started opening up. He began getting even more and more controlling and emotionally abusive. He was killing every bit of self-esteem in her always belittling her every action. He had also stopped coming with her to church for several months now.

One November day, while she was at a Sunday church service alone and the pastor was preaching, Anna could not help but talk to God. She could hear the pastor in the background but she was into her conversation with God.

"You don't love me. I have wanted nothing more growing up than to have a simple life and be happily married. I am married alright but look at what I am going through. I am alone. It's even almost Christmas time. My family is far away and the thoughts in my head are that of divorce. Where are You when I need You?" Anna kept grousing on and on.

Her conversation with God was interrupted by a loud unusual noise, even the whole church service including the pastor stopped. She looked up and searched for where the peculiar sound was coming from. She saw a lady standing amidst the church seats far left to where she was seated uttering unintelligible sounds. The lady went on for about thirty or forty seconds. When it was over, a lady, this time from the other side of the church building, stood up. She saw one of the church elders hand the microphone to the lady. The lady spoke and said, "God is saying there is someone here right now and you think that God does not love you and has left you. He wants you to know He is with you always and sees what you are going through. Do what you have to do for He says He loves you." The lady stopped and sat back down.

Anna was freaked out. She has read something about other Christians being "gifted" upon receiving the Holy Spirit. It was as if the message was exactly for her. She had goose bumps all over her. She was beginning to tear up and was worried that others will know that the message was for her. It was the first time she had witnessed someone "speaking in tongues" and someone "interpreting." Still immature in her faith, she thought, "These people are freaks." She nonchalantly got up and quietly exited the building. She tried to forget the incident.

She was extremely terrified at the thought of being a divorced woman as there was no such thing in her country. If things did not work out between couples, the couple just stayed separated or they would get an annulment, which takes an act of congress, so to speak. She decided that it was what she was going to do. She filed for divorce.

He was taken aback. From the initial reaction of denial, he then became very angry. He never thought she had it IN her to leave. He thought things would always stay the same. He would always be able to tell her where to go, what to do, who she can and cannot talk to, how much money she can spend, etc. He harassed her to the point that she had to file a restraining order against him. During this period, she would cry at night at the realization that she had failed her parents because they engrained in her that a good woman is a married woman. She went to work everyday with a happy face so that no one would know what she was going through until the divorced was finalized.

If there was another thing she was good at, it was at how good she was in hiding her pain from others. She left him the house, one of their cars and most of their money. He was verbally abusive to her during their marriage and extremely controlling. She was only allowed to drive from work to home and vice versa. If someone was to drop her to the next exit, she would not know how to go home as cars did not have built-in GPS system or Garmin at the time.

Even then, she still agreed to have his record expunged when he begged her to do so. He said that his reputation would get smeared. He told her that he had filed for citizenship.

All she wanted was freedom. She knew deep down inside, as long as she was willing to work, it is only a matter of time before she would accumulate enough to be able to send money to her family again. She just wanted out and so she did.

# Chapter 4

## The Second Fall

It was not until after a year or two post divorce, when she finally felt the courage to tell her parents that she had already been divorced. She did not want them to worry or feel her pain. She worried they might suffer medical and health risks if they were to find out.

Now, she is way over the situation and had already began healing and being able to talk about it without the flood of emotions that came with it. She also began sending her family money again on a regular basis.

Her failed marriage did not change her belief that marriage is a good thing. She began dating again and this time decided she was going to chose someone from the same religious background—Christian. Here enters Tommy, born and raised in a Christian household or so she thought. They met in one of the places where she worked. He lived in another state and despite the fact that she did not believe in long-distance relationships, they began dating.

### Tommy

Tommy was 6'2. He worked with computers. He was the person that anyone would talk to if they were having computer issues such as a frozen screen, invalid password, connection time out, etc. He traveled quite a bit as part of his job. He was bulky, Italian-looking and dressed well. He also shared Anna's love for trying different exotic foods and love for dancing.

They dated for a year. He then decided to move it to the next level. He proposed and decided it was best that they lived together as now they were engaged. Being the religious woman that she is, she prayed and asked for a sign. She thought of something highly unlikely to happen and asked THAT to be the sign.

She prayed,

*"God, I need a sign. If I should move in with this man, this is the sign I want. He never calls me at midnight. I need him to call me on this day at midnight, not 11:59pm not 12:01am but 12:00am. Midnight. Then I will know that Your answer is yes, and that I should move in with him."*

She knew in her heart God did not approve of cohabitating yet she arrogantly ordered God how she wanted things to be. Like a kid demanding a parent for a particular toy. At 12:01 am of the day she asked for the sign, the phone rang and it was Tommy. She looked at the clock and saw that it was 12:01. Deep down inside, Anna knew that the answer was a clear and definite "NO" but she stubbornly justified it in her mind because she wanted badly for the answer to be a yes. She said to her self, "It's only a minute difference, it couldn't hurt."

So she moved in with him. They "played house". They combined their finances like a married couple and that's when she realized he wasn't good with money, wasn't responsible and cannot be trusted.

"What was I thinking?" she said internally one day when she was alone in their apartment.

"We dated once a month for a year. That's only twelve dates!" she said to herself out loud.

"Who gets married after only twelve dates?"

"You. You fool!" She answered her self.

She saw that he was not used to having money and being able to afford nice things. It made him go crazy with spending knowing that now that he has money —Anna's money.

At least he is a Christian, is what she told herself to rationalize her choice to be with him when she started to question the decision she has made. Tommy was so selfish that even when one day, while he and Anna were walking in the mall and Anna gets approached by a stranger to be a model, instead of being flattered, Tommy enviously commented to Anna, "Why are they asking you to model? I am the one with a modeling background." Anna did not give it much thought as she did not want Tommy to get mad.

## The Worshipper

There was one thing that made Anna happy about her relationship with Tommy. He goes to church with her. They attended a very contemporary non-denominational church. The church building was huge. They had a live band and the church's dome provided great acoustics.

Tommy enjoyed all the praise and worship singing right before the preaching. However, Anna noticed that it almost always seemed every time there was an altar call, Tommy would go to the front, sometimes with tears and most of the time without, and would raise his hands up high in worship to the heavens and pray the prayer of acceptance almost every week.

Being immature in her faith, Anna would internally question why Tommy had to go to the front every altar call. She quietly asks her self, "If you accepted Christ once in your heart and meant it, does He leave and go out every Saturday that you have to ask him back in again the next Sunday?" She didn't understand.

## Winning the Lottery

After only 6 months of living together, he suggested that they get married. Although she had doubts, she agreed. She figured everyone has problems and that she was lucky to have a second chance. No marriage or relationship is perfect anyway, is what she said to console herself.

At 27, she didn't want a fancy wedding being that this wasn't her first. They had a simple civil wedding ceremony. Her income and his combined, though lower than her previous marriage, still added to about $100,000 /year. Not bad for a couple with no kids and no big mortgages to pay.

He started getting used to the idea that her money IS his money. Every weekend he would buy Italian clothing, car parts to transform his Honda to a "fast and furious" wannabe-car and video games and other electronic gadgets. He would hide things that he purchased with her money in the trunk of his car so that Anna would not know.

Since Anna did not balance their account to the dollar but instead in the hundreds, she only asked him to inform her of any purchase, if they were over a hundred dollars. She did not want to micromanage him. However, the devious in Tommy decided to always ask the cashier to ring each item separately so that no amount shows on the paper statement as over one hundred dollars at any given time. In his mind, this meant he could shop and spend $500 in one day and as long as the receipt or transaction appeared in their statement as being less than $100, he did not have to inform Anna. This Anna did not find out until much later.

With his prodding, they also eventually purchased a 4 bedroom house with 2 ½ bath and a Jacuzzi. It was beautiful. It was a federal style house with gray and black brick stone sidings and a two-car garage.

They bought nice and expensive furniture. Every room in the house had a theme. The master bedroom and bathroom had Egyptian décor. The guest bedroom had Greek theme, décor and furniture including naked sculptures of women for lamps. The room also had paintings pertinent to mythology, themes of man and his perfectibility.

The other guest bedroom had Mediterranean décor from the carpet to the wall mounts and beddings, wooden chest and bed frames. The family room and dining room had contemporary theme with minimalistic furniture from stores like Stylus and By Design. The formal living room had Japanese theme, red accent wall, black leather furniture and multiple samurai swords mounted on the wall.

One of his friends who came to visit him and Anna one day even jokingly asked, "Did you win the lottery man? What a house and a subservient wife! I am going to get me an Asian as well, if this is how it will be!"

Tommy stuck his Italian-German-descent-wannabe chest (because he always told people he was) out smugly in response.

She continued working to pay for everything as he, after almost a year of marriage, lost his job due to downsizing. She took another part-time job apart from her already-existing consulting part time. Anna was with a full time job, and two part-time jobs. She didn't have time for herself and had little to no rest.

She came home late most of the time because of all the traffic and job-juggling she had to do on a daily basis. Little did she know that he was purchasing a lot of 'stuff" without her knowledge. She has previously added him to all her credit cards and bank accounts. She didn't believe in having separate accounts because she believed that both spouses should know what "their" finances were. She also believed that to truly love another being, is to accept them for what they have, or don't have.

Later, she eventually found out, he had already accumulated at least $20,000 in credit card debts. He had also asked her for $9,000 tuition the month before telling her that he wanted to get certain computer program certifications. She felt bad because he has been unemployed for about a year and that his unemployment might be affecting his self-esteem so she reluctantly agreed. However, after Anna paid the tuition, he soon changed his mind and decided he was no longer interested in further studies and that it was now too late to get a refund. He figured she made good money and didn't bother to even address the matter with her. He was very irresponsible, unappreciative and arrogant.

The same qualities mentioned above, were the reasons for why he was one of the first ones to be let go by his company during a down-sizing. He could not find another job for two years and had to claim unemployment benefits. As is to be expected, he did not use the unemployment checks to help her with their household expenses. Instead, he left Anna to continue to work to pay for their debts, his school loans, their mortgage, etc.

Anna believed that in marriage, one should love their spouse "through thick or thin". She was so busy with work that she was coming home late most nights. He tells her that he had been busy looking for jobs but she saw that he continued to spend and live the same extravagant lifestyle— buy expensive clothes, frequently go out to eat even when he was not bringing in any income.

## Wolverine

One day, as he was out with one of his friends, Anna was at home off from work, when she heard a voice inside her telling her to go in the computer and check on what he had been up to. She was a believer in trust between married couples. Though she hesitantly sat in front of the computer, she began referring to herself in the third person reprimanding Anna herself saying, "This is not good Anna. You shouldn't be going through his stuff. They are his work stuff! Besides, working with computers is what he does for a living! You actually think you can go through his stuff without having his password?"

Her own thoughts made her queasy. She stayed seated in the office chair in front of the computer.

She tried to guess the password by trying different things—her birthday, his birthday, his mom's maiden name, their dog's name, his school, etc but none worked. She repeatedly saw, "Invalid password". In frustration, she sighed and said out loud, "I told you this won't work!" She was again talking to God, her ethereal friend.

Feeling stupid, she decided to stop. She got up to do something productive. All of a sudden, the word "WOLVERINE" popped in her head. She laughed and in disbelief said, "Wolverine? What's wolverine?" She typed it anyway. What do you know? Viola! The screen opened up to his email filled with inboxes, pictures and messages to and from other women. She read through them and realized that his "job search" was more "mate search". He had been telling women that he was single and working. She was nauseated, dizzy and trembling.

"What the hell do you think you are doing?" she heard him speak from behind her.

Startled, she responded, "What's all these?"

He turned it on her saying that she is invading his privacy. He justified it by saying he was bored and just needed something to do. He added, "You're never home!" in an effort to deflect it on her.

As she got up from her chair, she proceeded to ran to the garage in tears saying, "This is not right! I'm leaving!" He chased her and muscled her away from the door . He pinned her down on the floor in one of the submission moves that he knows from his martial arts training. He told her she was going nowhere. He added that as a Christian wife, she needs to listen to her husband and do what he, her husband, says.

"Ok, ok, I'm sorry. Now can you let me go?" Anna asked. It was the only way she knew how to get out alive. Later that night, he apologized and said that he did not appreciate her invading his privacy. He adds, "I love you but it's just you. You provoke me. Don't do it again ok?"

"OK," Anna said when in her mind but inside it translated as, "What a jerk!"

## The Bruises

This is not the first time he had laid hands on her. He had done it at least seven other times. Every time she disagreed with him or had a different opinion or asked where their money went, she earned bruises as dark purple as eggplants. But with her intelligence level, she feared everyone will make fun of her because of her poor decisions, including that of being with Tommy.

She decided she would make up stories at work saying she bumped into a furniture or what not, if anyone at work noticed or asked about the mysterious bruises.

One day while at work one of Anna's co-worker noted the bruises on her arms.

"What are those from?" the co-worker inquired pointing to her bruises.

"Oh nothing," Anna responded trying to terminate the conversation.

"How did you get them?" the co-worker insisted.

"I was cleaning and I bumped into the table," Anna fabricated.

"You must have an unusual piece of table in your house," the co-worker remarked sarcastically to indicate that she knew Anna was fibbing.

"Yeah, I guess," Anna agreed and tried to leave the room pretending to head to her next patient.

Depending on how mad Tommy was, the act can vary from a push to the tub or the floor, being dragged on the kitchen floor or having his fingers shoved into her mouth symbolically telling her to shut her mouth up and not to ever dare talk back to him. He manipulated her and used her fear of God to make her stay in such an abusive relationship. He always told her it was her fault.

She remembers him being so paranoid one day that when she had tried to leave, he disconnected something in her car's engine without her knowing so she could not drive off during a fight. It scared her that if she died, there would be no one to inform her family and no one to take care of her them. A fear so deep that she always obliged to Tommy just to calm things down and end his rage.

## 411/911

During one of their many fights, she tried to call 911 for fear of being killed but then rescinded on her decision as she internalized that maybe she really is the problem. Plus her stupid heart told her she would be a very bad wife if she sent her husband in prison and did not try to work things out.

Anna heard the doorbell ring. She opened the door and saw a no-nonsense female cop.

"Ma'am we received a 911 call from this address," the female officer said.

"Oh I am so sorry. I was dialing 411 trying to look for a number, "Anna confabulated for fear of Tommy being thrown to jail.

"I see that one of your car doors was left open," the officer continued. "Were you trying to leave?"

"Oh no ma'am", Anna fibbed. "I was trying to get groceries in and may have forgotten to push one of the car doors hard enough after I was done bringing in the groceries."

"It looks like you have been crying. Is everything ok?" the officer persistently continued.

"Yes ma'am, everything is ok," she heard herself lie.

"I was cutting up some onions earlier before the doorbell rang that's why I look like I had been crying," Anna fabricated some more.

"Well give us a call should you need further assistance," the exasperated officer said.

"I sure will," Anna retorted.

The cop's visit quickly calmed Tommy down, and he acted nicely towards Anna at least for the rest of that day.

## Dr. Phil

It was only a matter of time before another fight ensued. Anna remembers accidentally watching a Dr. Phil show one day and the topic was about abusive relationships and abusive men. She recalls one of the battered women being interviewed and being asked why they stay in such relationships as saying, "well he apologizes after we fight and tells me he loves me and that he only did so because I provoked him."

It was as if she heard what Tommy usually tells her after beating her up—that he was truly sorry and that it would not have happened had she not made him get so angry. "I am like these women," Anna painfully realized.

Tommy always got physical and abusive whenever he does not get his way. This one time, however, Anna was no longer scared of dying. Tommy had beaten her up and dragged her ass many times before. She learned that though the physical marks go away over time, she is always left with the emotional and mental bruises.

She remembered being angry with God at how He gave her yet another man far bigger and much more physically and emotionally abusive than the previous one. What's worse is that, he even claimed to be a Christian. At least the other one grew up and was taught by his culture not to value women so he didn't know any better, is what she thought. When she mustered enough strength and breath to speak while Tommy's fingers were still shoved in her mouth during a fight, she uttered, "Go ahead. Kill me. Do it. You will do me a big favor."

In shock, as this was the first time she did not act scared, Tommy stopped and composed himself to apologize to her. He said, "I'm sorry. I'll never do it again. It's just you. You provoke me. You should listen to me more next time." She agreed, as she has always done in the past, but in her mind, this time she came up with a plan.

Realizing that trying to leave him when he is mad always leads to her being beaten up more or her car engine being broken so she could not drive off, she decided she had to make it seem like it was HIS idea. She had to boost his ego. That's how he always operated anyway, she thought to herself.

## Mom's student

The Saturday of their most recent squabble started out seeming like any other Saturdays they have had before. Anna usually wakes up around ten and Tommy usually wakes up later around noon. Saturday was Anna's house cleaning day.

Anna walked down the stairs and headed to the kitchen to make her self a pot of coffee. She likes being productive even on the days she is off from work. As the coffee maker started brewing, Anna began opening all their wooden blinds to let the light in. It was clear and bright outside. Anna loves looking outside. It always gave her peace.

The smell of coffee filled the kitchen. She was pouring herself a cup when she heard Tommy's footsteps coming down the stairs.

"Morning," Anna greeted as she noticed Tommy all dressed up.

"Morning," he replied.

"Why are you up so early?" Anna inquired.

"My friend Mel and I are going to a car show. I forgot to tell you," he informed.

He leaned over to kiss her goodbye and went out the door.

Not long after Tommy left, Anna's cell phone started ringing. She saw "mom" on the phone screen as it lay on top of their kitchen island. She picked up and heard a familiar voice.

"Hi Ma! How are you?"

"I'm okay. How are you?"

Anna during her tumultuous relationship with Tommy never spoke a word of it to her mom or anyone in her family for that matter. Every time they talked, Anna always said everything was okay. She did not say anything bad about Tommy to her coworkers, friends or family. No one even knew he was unemployed. More importantly, no one knew about him hurting her. Anna did not want anyone she cared for, especially her parents, worrying over her.

"Are you telling me the truth?" her mother asked.

"Of course I am. Why would you ask me that?" Anna surprisingly responded.

"I have a student who has some kind of gift. People come to her for help and ask her questions. She is known for very accurate answers and predictions. She never takes money and she's a good girl. She saw me this week. She apologized to me and said that what she will tell me next might be painful for me to hear. I listened. She told me that you are being beaten up by your husband. She said you don't tell us anything because you don't want us to worry."

As her mother kept talking, Anna's knees got weak and she sat down on the kitchen floor. She felt tears running down her cheeks. She didn't know what to say so she didn't answer. She was asking herself, "How could that person have known? I don't know her."

"Is that true?" Anna heard her mother ask.

Anna's lips quivered as she tried to speak. "I am so sorry Ma. I don't know what's wrong? Why does it keep happening to me? What have I done to deserve this? I am not a bad person," she confided sobbing uncontrollably.

"I know. I know. Please leave. You have my blessing. I don't want to get a phone call telling me you're dead. I know we are far and can't help you. Please leave." Her mother begged.

"I will Ma. I can't talk anymore. I'm sorry. I love you," Anna said

"I love you too," her mother replied before Anna hung up.

Anna went back to bed and wept. "What did I do to You to deserve this? I have tried to be nothing but good. I thought You blessed me by allowing me to be married again and to a Christian nonetheless. What a Christian he turned out to be? Why do You seem to take pleasure in punishing me? I see You really love me alright?" She was angry at God. She cried and cried for hours by herself until she fell asleep.

## No Fear

In the following weeks and days, she pretended to be the same subservient wife. Whenever there was a change in her work schedule or free time, she looked for apartments for him. It had to be in a "yuppie" neighborhood and a fairly expensive one so he would agree to move. He was all about "showing off".

When she had finally found a place for him, she paid three months' rent in advance and told him how she felt bad that she was causing him so much grief and making him mad.

She also told him that she thinks he was right in saying that they may be in some need of time apart and explained how she found a nice place close to his work that he would really like. He never really suggested anything to that effect but Anna was so convincing that Tommy really thought it was his idea to begin with. She even offered for him to take to the apartment whatever furniture in their house he likes, so he can be as comfortable as possible. He looked at the place, liked it and agreed to move.

She helped him organize the apartment and make it as much of a bachelor's pad as possible. He loved it. He believed it was his idea. How? Who knows? All that mattered to Anna was that soon he will be out of the house.

As soon as they had finished moving him and everything else he wanted into to the apartment, she went home, quickly changed the locks and subsequently filed for divorce. Much like her "first fall", she just wanted to leave and start over again. She told her female lawyer to not divide the credit card debts he incurred and just leave it as her responsibility so that he will not dispute the divorce and prolong it. She felt like Tina Turner, she just wanted her freedom. She even gave him their already paid-for (by her) Honda S1 convertible. To her, all that mattered is that she got out alive and away from the 6'2" killing machine ball-and-chain. His zodiac sign was cancer and what a cancer he turned out to be indeed.

As they were waiting for the divorce to be finalized, he begged her to reconsider. Using her religious background against her, he convinced her that they need to seek counseling from church before they give up on their marriage.

She felt bad. He was right. They did not ask help from the church initially so she eventually conceded. She wanted to make sure she did every thing she can to make it work.

They went to counseling for at least 2 months. Shortly thereafter, however, she realized that it was all a waste of time. Whenever they were in a counseling session, he would tell the church elders that she did not listen to him as a Christian wife should. He also completely denied the fact that he physically abused her, stole their tax refund money and lied about it, cheated and pretended to be single among other things. Because the messages that the elders were getting were inaccurate based on Tommy's one —sided statements, their counseling were erroneous as well. Instead of Tommy being counseled not to be physically abusive, it was Anna who was being told to be more understanding and forgive Tommy for beating her up. She decided to proceed with the divorce and "stop all the nonsense." She did not feel the need to tell the elders her side of the story. He is never going to change, she concluded.

When she finally received the signed divorce papers, she felt as though a ton of weight was lifted off her shoulders and she let out of her a great big sigh of relief. She decided that time, no more Christian men and no more to church.

# Chapter 5

## The Third Fall

After dusting herself off from her most recent fall, Anna started her life again. She went out with friends and did not date anybody seriously. For about two years she learned or tried to, at least, love being by herself. Her experience with her wife-beating so-called-Christian ex-husband left her very angry at God. She didn't pray or go to church anymore in the years that followed. She was by herself. Alone with no one but herself, she did not want to be good anymore. She told herself that getting to know and being closer to God just means more trials and more trials mean more pain and sorrow.

### Miguel

In June of 2006, she met this man Miguel. He was nothing like the men she had dated in the past. She likes tall bulky men. He was tall and skinny. He also wasn't keen on fashion. But somehow, they got along well when it comes to talking about everyday topics. He also was not a Christian. A big plus, Anna thought. Because she wasn't physically attracted to him in the beginning and had even categorized him, in her mind, as in the "only-friends" basket, she didn't see him anything being other than a friend.

But Miguel was very persistent. Anna did like the fact that Miguel never made any sexual advances, not by chat, text or email. They just always talked about life in general. She saw that he was a little pessimistic but she rationalized it as Miguel just being realistic.

One day, after two months of correspondence via internet on an almost daily basis, he asked if he could meet Anna in person. She agreed only because she thought he was very persistent and seemingly "harmless." When he met Anna in person, he instantly fell in love with her. He told her later, after they were married, that when they met for dinner for the first time, he knew he wanted to marry her. Within two months of dating, he fell head over heels in love with her.

To Miguel, Anna was extremely different from all other women he had dated. She didn't seem preoccupied with impressing him even though he thought he was a "good catch." He considered himself good looking and at that time he was already working as a manager at the Cheesecake Factory, a well known restaurant.

Miguel saw how Anna loves life and didn't seem to "need" a man. Anna was just Anna . . . . fun-loving and carefree.

Anna, on the other hand, was doing her best to show Miguel all her bad qualities. The Anna created by life's beating. Soon after her divorce from Tommy, Anna changed her ways. She started drinking, going and staying out late with her girlfriends, doing anything she could do so that Miguel would not want to try to take their relationship to the next level. But he did anyway.

## The proposal

The night Miguel proposed, Anna remembered wanting to have some "me" time. Miguel stopped by that day at her apartment wanting to see her after she had left work.

Anna came home tired and immediately went to the bathroom to take a shower while Miguel watched TV waiting for Anna. When Anna stepped out of the shower, she then proceeded to spot her blemishes with Clearasil hoping to go to bed earlier than usual. She had white dots all over her face but was too exhausted to think of how Miguel would react if he was to see her that way.

As she came out of the bathroom, Miguel knelt down in front of her holding a box.

"I would love for you to be my wife," he said as he flipped open the box for Anna to see.

It was a yesterday-today-tomorrow three stone engagement kind of ring. It sparkled.

"Oh, no!" This is not the proposal I had in mind. My hair is not being blown by the wind nor do I have make up on," is the internal dialogue she had in her head. But being the hopeless romantic that she is, despite her two failed relationships, she again said "yes".

## Polar Opposites

Although thankful that she doesn't seem to have any problems with having men propose to her, Anna was feeling down. She is beginning to see herself very unlucky in love. She accepted yet another serious relationship. She loved him but was not IN LOVE with him. She figured she always wanted bulky testosterone-high men (somehow equating it with manliness) and figured Miguel was skinny and less assertive or aggressive. She wondered if she finally figured the formula for a successful marriage. Nevertheless, she wanted to give it a try.

Within six months of dating, they soon got engaged and got married thereafter. Anna saw weddings as only a "one day' event and as such opted for the easy civil wedding yet again. She believed that "marriage is a lifetime" and therefore thought that the "wedding ceremony" should not be the high point of any relationship.

She and Miguel were polar opposites—she loved life . . . he was reclusive. On the days she wants to dress up, he wants to dress down. She believed in having nice stuff believing that she will always have and always be able to afford nice things while he believed in always saving for "rainy days." Not that Anna squandered her money but she always knew where her supply came from . . . . God, her ethereal friend. She always knew it in her core, even when she was angry at Him and tried not to acknowledge it. Anna's desire to give alms to the poor also led to frequent disagreements.

## Tithing

Whenever Anna feels sad or unhappy with her relationship with Miguel, God comes to mind.

The thought of God brought Anna to memory lane from years ago. She remembered when she first started attending a non-denominational church in her country which she did in secret as her family members were devout Catholics. It was called, "Praise Cathedral". She was still in college then.

She sat in the church pew one Sunday, listening to a sermon about tithing.

In the Catholic Church, they were told to give what they can. She had just received her first paycheck as a full time therapist earlier that week. She gave almost all of her money to her mom to help out with the family's monthly expenses. Now, here she is listening to a new teaching about having to give a tenth of her earnings to God. She looked down at the money she had pulled from her pocket and realized that the amount that was left, after the family's bills had been paid, amounted to about one tenth of her pay. She saw the envelop where tithes and offerings were to be placed as she heard part of the preaching being some verse from the book of Malachi, "try Me in this . . . and see if I will not throw open the floodgates of heaven and pour out so much blessing there won't be room to contain it."

"But if I give you these, which is a tenth of what I have, I won't have money to go home?" she asked God without uttering a word. She hurriedly put the money in the envelope and placed it in the bucket being passed around before she was tempted to hold on to it.

With her hands on her lap, she reminded God, "Ummmm . . . now You've got a problem. I have no money with me so You'll have to find a way to get me home. I have three rides to take—jeep, train and then jeep again." As if God didn't know her circumstances.

She sat and waited in the same pew until one of the elders ushered everyone that it was time to go as they had to clean and prepare for the next service. She had no choice but to sit and wait outside though she really had no clue what she was waiting for.

Out of nowhere she heard, "Hi Anna. How are you? I have been wanting to see you!" She was someone she met in one of the youngsters Saturday church services a few months ago. She couldn't even remember her name.

"I'm fine, thank you," she politely replied. She was never in the habit of telling people any of her problems.

"I wanted to give you back the money I owed you,' the youngster said.

"What money? You don't owe me anything," she quickly retorted.

"Yes I did. Here take it. Thank you. Sorry but I gotta go. Good to see you!"

Before she could reply, the young girl was gone and left her with money that amounted to the exact fare she needed for the first jeep ride. She still had no recollection of when the girl had borrowed money from her. Nevertheless, she was thankful and under her breath smilingly said, "Now just two more rides."

The jeep ride brought her to the train station. When she got there, she sat down contemplating what she can do to get on the train. As she began to think, she heard a male voice yelling in the crowd, "Anna, Anna."

She looked up to find a familiar face. Her cousin Jeric, who is an engineer and who she has not seen in months, came up to her and asked, "What are you doing here?"

"Oh just waiting," she said nonchalantly. She didn't want to elaborate as she didn't like being pitied or asking money from others.

"Well I am on my way home but take this. I had just closed a contract recently," he said as he pulled bills from his wallet and handed them to her. He, too, seemed in a hurry and before she could count the money and say thank you, he had sped off and got on the train.

When she finally counted the bills, she realized she had more than enough money not only for the train and next jeep ride to make it home but even had a couple hundred pesos left to use for the next two weeks. "Thank you Lord," she said quietly in her mind but the skeptical side of her let out,

"Hhhmmmnn?" as she looked at the money in her hand and shook her head in disbelief.

## Many Firsts

Things went well for Miguel and Anna for the first two years. Miguel came from a poor family and had an alcoholic and bipolar for a mother growing up. His father died in the army service while he was still only six. His grandfather was the only solid male figure in his life. Something about Anna loved taking care of others who she thought had difficult lives.

Anna exposed Miguel to many "firsts" as she felt bad for him for having a difficult childhood. She took him to places and restaurants he had never been before and encouraged him to do and try different experiences. She took him to Sea World and Disneyland in Florida, Atlantis in the Bahamas, Rock City and Ruby Falls in Tennessee, and The Aquarium to name a few. She introduced him to white water rafting, parasailing, swimming with the dolphins, going to live hockey, basketball and football events with good seats, to concerts etc.

She gave him some "culture". Before her, Miguel's life included going to McDonald's on Friday nights as his idea of "splurging" on himself. He was still with student and car loans when they met.

Anna never believed in having debts. She always tried to pay her credit card balances in full and never bought things that she couldn't pay for. She was also good in saving money but never to the point of being a miser. Somehow, her Christian learning from way back when always stuck. She always remembered a verse saying, " . . . the head and not the tail . . . above and not below . . . . lenders not borrowers."

Anna always gave to others even when she ran away from God. She believed that it is in giving that we receive. In the two years with Miguel, they had accumulated about $140,000. Anna worked long hours as a manager and knew how to balance between "living life" and "saving for the future".

Being that she was busy with work, she left the finances to Miguel. Anna was always very trusting. Unfortunately, the longer Miguel had been in charge with the finances, the more strict and obsessed he became with money.

Even though Anna was the breadwinner and he was a full time student during the third year of their marriage, Miguel started telling Anna what she could and could not spend her money on. If she needed clothes and would buy a few items for herself in Wal-Mart or Target to make Miguel happy, which she never did before meeting Miguel as she always previously shopped in stores like Neiman Marcus, Macy's , Express and Banana Republic, he still would say something to her about the purchase.

He was obsessed with trying to save and being millionaires in the next 10 years knowing how much Anna made.

## Wal-Mart

Anna came home one day with a $30 purchase from Wal-Mart. It has been at least four months since she's bought something for herself. She also felt elated that she did not spend much and now has two new blouses for the cost of $30. You did good, she told herself. She recalls buying blouses in the past which cost twice or thrice the amount she spent today just for one blouse.

"Look what I got," Anna exclaimed as she excitedly took the items from the bag.

"You bought another blouse?" Miguel responded even before seeing how much it cost or what it looks like.

"You didn't even see what it looks like," Anna retorted. She was trying her best not to get in a fight and just brush off Miguel's comment. "It's only thirty dollars," Anna added.

"But didn't you just buy a blouse four months ago?" Miguel kept on.

Anna did not reply. She headed towards the bedroom, changed to some house clothes and proceeded to cook. She remained quiet the rest of the night.

## Color Blind

Miguel's lack of appreciation for all of Anna's support and love made her cry in silence on most nights. She remembers that it seemed better when Miguel didn't know how much she made. She remembers him being humble and a little more appreciative then. Even though she was realizing she was unhappy, she did not want to leave. How could she? This is her third go at it.

Miguel is color blind and she remembered how he would pair certain dress shirts with certain ties thinking that they matched because he was seeing a totally different color in his head. Anna, knowing a little about fashion, felt bad for him and took it upon herself to number the ties and the dress shirts that went well with it so that Miguel would know which shirt should go with which tie. He initially thought her color combinations were bad being colorblind but started realizing how well Anna's choices made him look when he started getting more compliments. He was getting compliments from men and women alike. He also received plenty of compliments from women he found or thought of as pretty or with some fashion sense, on the evenings when he worked at the restaurant. He began even asking Anna, whenever they would get ready to go anywhere on the weekends, to pick his clothes out for him.

## Angelina

Anna was always very loving, trusting and kind. Everything that she has, she always gave to others around her. She always felt compelled to pick and take others that other people won't take.

When she was in college and the instructor would tell the students to pair up for an activity, even when she was asked by others to pair up with them, she would decline and pair up with whoever was left and not asked by anyone else. She always felt the need to root for the underdog in any situation or competition. It was this same compulsion that made her meet her friend Angelina.

Anna usually went to LA fitness to exercise when she did get a chance.

One day while waiting for the class to start, she noticed a lady in a corner all by herself. All other ladies had cliques and little groups of people they talked with while waiting for the instructor. Anna had been going to those classes for a while and knew a number of women who greeted her with a smile or waved at her whenever she walked in.

No one was talking to this lady. Being the kind person that she is, she initiated a conversation with the lady.

"Habla espanol?" Anna asked with her elementary Spanish.

"Si!" the lady responded with a smile as if finally happy to get to talk to someone.

"Me llamo Anna. Y tu?" Anna continued.

"Angelina." The lady replied.

They continued their conversation and soon became friends. Angelina was new to the US and did not have close friends at the time. As they got to know one another better, they started going out together once a month as they both liked to dance.

Miguel never liked seeing Anna dressed up as he knew she always attracted men's attention. Going out with Angelina, even though it was only once a month, made Miguel very upset. Anna and Miguel would always end up having a fight when Anna came home because he felt he was loosing his control on her. Anna used to always do as he bided—not have any friends, only go where he wanted her to, only spend how much he would allow her to etc, etc.

By the end of their third year together, he was getting resentful that Anna brought more money to the household than he ever did. He tells Anna, "you and your work friends live in a bubble." He also use to get mad at Anna for always wanting to help or give something to somebody she thought was in need. He would sarcastically say, "who are we giving presents or money to this week?"

Anna recalls her shock when he decided to go back to school and surprised her with the news of him going to therapy school since he seemed to hate her line of work.

"I am going back to school to become a therapist. I quit my job today,"

Anna doesn't recall a discussion regarding the matter but wanted to be supportive so she just said okay and thought maybe he did mention it to her and she just forgot. She encouraged him by saying she will support him every step of the way.

They have a decent relationship is what Anna thought. She believed that no marriage is perfect and that the pair had to just learn to compromise. And compromise she did.

All Anna wanted was to be happy.

When they got together in the beginning, Anna had just taken an offer at work to be in a management position. Miguel initially seemed supportive but later resented the fact that Anna always made more than he did. He has learned over the years that somehow Anna always had God's financial favor even when to Miguel's eyes she did not appear "holy and pure." Instead of seeing Anna as a teammate, being that she was married to him, Miguel always saw Anna as his competition.

Miguel's despise for Anna's "favor" grew more and more each day. It was as if he was hoping things would stop going well for Anna. He gets annoyed when a relative, friend or co-worker thinks that Anna was younger than him even though she was 3 years older. He gets envious when Anna would bring home trophies or awards she received at work— associate of the quarter, best team of the quarter, manager of the quarter etc.

## Jaden

Anna, prior to knowing God, was quite pessimistic. If there was something that could go wrong, Anna expected it to happen to her. It wasn't until after she met Jaden, that she started believing in the power of words. She learned it from him when they briefly dated years ago.

Jaden was a few years older than Anna when they met. He worked in advertising and flipped houses on the side. Jaden was very generous and nature loving. Anna saw it in how carefully he would water his plants, how he would thank God and "the universe" for a beautiful day, how he always stayed calm.

Jaden lived in a high rise condo in the wealthier and "old money" areas of the city. He had a very active social life. He was always in events or seminars. He never seemed to worry about money. She remembers how he had asked her if she wanted front row tickets to a concert one day and she mistakenly thought he was offering her drugs.

He left a message on her voicemail, "Crystal meth this Thursday?"

Anna was furious. How can he even think she was into drugs? She was so mad that left him a message saying, "How dare you think I do drugs? I don't want to see you or hear from you ever again!"

Jaden called her back later and told her that he was referring to the band Crystal Meth who was in town that week. He told her to check the entertainment section of the newspaper so she would know he wasn't lying. Anna did and yes, Jaden did not lie. Anna apologized.

One day, during one lunch date with Anna and Jaden conversing, Anna had commented how she has a part time job because she needed extra income.

"Anna, you don't NEED extra income, you DESERVE extra income," he quickly corrected Anna.

"There is power in your words you know?" he continued.

Annoyed and finding Jaden to sound a little preachy, she began to loose interest in him. She thought to herself, "What does he know of needing anyway? He has an easy life. He has money and can work from home. He's in a bubble and we have nothing in common. He is rich and I am from the working class. We have nothing in common"

She never answered his calls again though the words he had said and how he was towards life left an impression on her that she wouldn't realize until much later.

## The Tax Return

"Miguel, I am seeing a five digit return on our taxes," Anna claimed.

"Are you insane? We don't have kids and you make a good income. We would be paying. I am sure." Miguel quickly negatively countered.

"No. Don't say that. We have been diligent in paying our taxes. Why do you always claim bad things for us?" Anna rhetorically asked, saddened by Miguel's comment.

They both remained quiet as they knew it would just end up in an argument if anyone of them continued. Anna organized all their receipts and paystubs and later on that week filed taxes jointly.

Anna was at worked when she received a call from Miguel. Being that Miguel never called at work, Anna figured it was an emergency.

"Are you sitting down?" Miguel inquired.

"No. Why?" she asked as she started looking for a chair and proceeded to sit down bracing herself for Miguel's next statement.

"You are right! The accountant said we are getting at least $10,000 back," he excitedly reported.

"Oh my God! You scared me. But yes that is great news. Now you see? Maybe it could have been more if you didn't negate my statements," she sarcastically remarked.

Anna quickly ended the conversation reminding Miguel that she had to get back to work.

During their marriage, Anna also taught Miguel about day trading. She told him to watch the Bloomberg channel and to take down notes on which companies are being bought or sold, any new medications out in the market, any new product that a company maybe launching. She taught him how acquisitions and mergers affect quarterly earnings and projections. With her guidance, Miguel made at least $20,000 in day trading even while he was full time in school. However, when Miguel would tell others of his success in day trading, there was no mention of Anna teaching him the ropes. It was all because of his own intelligence.

## Envy

Angelina and Anna continued to be friends. When they would go out, Angelina noticed how they always got "good treatment". Anna always seemed to be liked by the manager or owner of the restaurant or places they visited and always had good seats or table. Angelina liked feeling special but in her heart envied how Anna seemed to have it all—beauty, brains and favor.

Angelina, Anna later realized, was very unhappy in her marriage. When Anna had asked why she would not leave, Angelina admitted she had applied for her green card.

Even though she did not approve of it, whenever Angelina would tell her about a man she is cheating with, Anna did not say a word to Angelina's husband or to her husband Miguel. She did not want to make matters worse knowing that Miguel doesn't like her going out with Angelina anyway. She did not feel the need to meddle with Angelina's life. To her, they are friends but their lives are their own lives to live.

They remained friends for about two years and Anna kept all of Angelina's cheating exploits to herself.

# Chapter 6

## The Dusk

### Meeting Sonny

During one of Anna and Angelina's night out, Anna met Sonny. He was a skinny young bartender. He had served them previously before with their favorite drink—long island iced tea. Anna never really talked to him.

Sonny had an unusual hairstyle. He was one of those Anna described as "gothic looking." He was very quiet but polite to customers. Anna had noticed how fast and efficient he is and how he does not seem to flirt with women like most bartenders do. She thought he was harmless.

One day, Sonny had invited her to come to a band rehearsal. During the invite,

Anna found out that Sonny played in a band. He told her that their band's goal is to create music and songs that uplifted women. He told her they were looking for a face that would represent the band. They wanted a face that is socially ambiguous since they want their music to touch women from different races from all walks of life. They asked if she would consider being the "face" for the band. Anna liked the music concept of lifting women's spirit.

They started maintaining correspondence via text. Although part of Anna's being told her that it was not a good idea, she felt a certain happiness with Sonny's positivity. Something she wished Miguel would give her.

She learned more about Sonny's life and realized he was poor and was homeless for months, a year before they met, following his music dreams. He told her that he slept at the music studio. He also told her how he would go sometimes go to Subway to buy a cookie just so he can sit on one of the tables and pretend to read a newspaper so he can sleep. He also told her how he walked or rode the MARTA to get to work. She admired that he dreamed big. He believed he was going to be a star one day.

## The Night at the Bar

It may have began as pity but Anna's compassion towards Sonny gradually changed. She found herself one night agreeing to go out to have a drink even though she was still, at the time, married to Miguel.

They went to a bar where they had live music. They had drinks, talked about Sonny's dreams, danced and enjoyed good music. Nothing else happened.

As Anna walked towards the restroom to freshen up, Sonny walking by her side as he was headed to the men's room as well, a lady commented, "You two are a lovely couple. You look like you guys should be on TV," she complimented. They politely said thank you and each went inside their respective restrooms. When they left the bar, Anna dropped Sonny off to his apartment complex.

She hurried home so she wouldn't get in so much trouble with Miguel. She made it home around two and Miguel was already fast asleep.

Anna convinced herself that she would stop responding to Sonny's texts. She didn't want to jeopardize her already shaky marriage. Little did she realize that Miguel had been reading all her texts and knew all along about Sonny. Even when Miguel admitted that the texts he read were mainly empty talks of two people encouraging one another or talking about dreams and staying positive, he still felt furious and cheated. It reminded him that he was losing control over Anna. Because of his fear with not having money, Miguel decided it was best that he divorce Anna and attribute it to her "cheating by text" so he could keep the house and half of all their savings even though he was mainly unemployed and a full time student for most of their marriage.

Internalizing and blaming herself for even allowing her self to engage in texting and even go out one time with another man, Anna felt Miguel was right. It suddenly hit her. This is her third marriage and she's again headed for divorce. She felt so ashamed that she wished the earth would just swallow her whole. Miguel was out of town visiting his grandpa.

## The Pills

Anna decided she would try to end it all. She figured she was lucky to have had proposals from each of the first three boyfriends she's had . . . three marriages. How stupid was that? "You nincompoop!" she told herself. "Maybe you missed your calling. You should have been a basketball player judging by how good you are with "rebounds," she continues to belittle her self. She tried to make herself feel better by telling her self that some women never even get at least one marriage proposal in their time. "They also did not get abused like her three times by three different men," said the sarcastic side of her. She worried, "What man would love you now? Even J Lo with her big booty, money and looks is sometimes seen as a loser by others because of her failed marriages. And she is famous. You are nobody. You are not even anything like her. You don't have her money, her looks, much less her booty."

Deep down inside, Anna knew that God did not approve of anyone trying to take the life He had given them. Anna spoke to her self and said, "You're not trying to do anything bad. You just want to sleep and not wake up. It's not like there will be blood or anything. Besides, no one would get hurt."

Anna convinced her self and soon ingested ten sleeping pills. She did not want to take more pills as the vain part of her worried about how her remains would look like in the casket if her body hardened with her foaming at the mouth. The mere visual image of it made her cringe.

"Ten would be good. You would look like you just left in peace," she assured her self.

Anna felt her consciousness soon fading away. It will finally be over is what she thought.

Fifteen hours had passed since Anna took the pills. As she lay in bed, she started hearing a sound. It slowly got louder and louder. A part of her consciousness was coming back and she began to question, "Would I wake up to heaven or hell?"

As the sound got clearer, she started opening her eyes slowly. She soon learned that she was in the same bed waking up to the sound of the ceiling fan as it rotated.

"God damn it! I'm still here? F—k!" she blurted.

"Dang pills!" she continued.

"Even with death, I can't get a break," she muttered as she headed downstairs to find food. She was starving.

## The Third Miss

She agreed to begin the divorce process and decided to leave. She's so unlucky she thought. She wondered how Angelina seemed so lucky that she could keep cheating with several different men and never get caught. She almost wished she had been intimate with Sonny so at least the divorce would have been worth it. She never got to test drive the car, she thought.

Anna kept her word, even when she and Miguel separated and were waiting for the divorce to be final, she kept supporting Miguel and paid for his monthly mortgage and health insurance until he graduated from school and started working. She even helped him find a job. She promised Miguel, when they were still married, that she would support him until he graduated and she was determined to keep her word.

## Soulmates

Sonny upon learning of the separation, took advantage of the situation and opened to Anna about his feelings for her. Before long, she found herself living in with Sonny. Her she is again sinning, Anna thought.

Everything seemed perfect at first just like any love story. Sonny was very clean and helped around the apartment. He was very loving and did "sweet little things" to always make Anna feel special. He would leave her love notes or surprise her with a visit to her work with breakfast and flowers. He would bring her coffee as he knew she likes coffee in the mornings. He would cook whenever he can and most of all, always reminded her of how lucky he is to have found her.

Their work schedules were very different. Anna had an eight-to-five job and Sonny worked nights until around 3 am and would then head to the studio to practice. Sonny always tried to make it home by six so he could catch Anna before she headed off to work.

Anna always woke up to Sonny giving her a kiss and then kneeling on the side of the bed so he could lay his head by her chest. He would stay there and just hold her for a few minutes. He would then change to something more comfortable, make coffee and begin practicing. He appreciated Anna for paying for all their monthly expenses to help support his dream. Something his parents or family did not do for him.

Anna always admired Sonny's drive. No matter how exhausted he would be from work, any time that he has was always used wisely. We would help clean the apartment and then proceed to watching videos of guitar lessons to learn more chords or come up with rifts.

On the very few days that he is off from work, he would practice until his fingers were blistered. Anna remembers him telling her, "I like practicing especially until around two or three in the morning when most people are asleep. That's usually when I come up with the coolest rifts."

They seemed perfect for each other. Wherever they went, they always received compliments from strangers of how fashionable they were and how great they look together.

## At the Coffee Shop

They were also a match when it comes to loving the poor. Having been homeless a few months a year before meeting Anna, Sonny always had a soft spot for the homeless. Something she respected and loved about him.

It was during one afternoon they had met for coffee, even before she decided to move in with him, that she witnessed how giving Sonny was.

They were sitting outside of Starbucks somewhere downtown. Though the area where the coffee shop was brimming with city life and bustle, it was also filled with beggars and homeless people constantly panhandling. They were chatting away when a homeless gentleman approached their table and asked Sonny for money.

"Excuse me sir but can I bum a couple of bucks to buy some food?" the person asked.

Anna knew that Sonny was struggling to make ends meet and worked hard as a bartender to support his music dreams. Every dollar of tip he made mattered. Anna thought Sonny would ask the man to go away but instead, he took out his wallet and pulled out the cash that was in it and gave it to the man.

Without meaning to do so, Anna saw the exact amount—one five dollar bill and two ones. Seven dollars total was it. Yet, he took it all out and gave to the man. She did not say a word but his action made her have an internal conversation.

"I, too, am a generous and compassionate person. I make a decent income. I have given two, sometimes three dollars, to a beggar before as well. But I have never given more than that and it was never ALL I had," she reflected.

Almost condescendingly she asked, "Why would you give him everything you have? You are struggling yourself," she pointed out as if he did not already know.

"It never hurts to help others. It takes a lot to ask a total stranger for money," he calmly replied. "The universe will pay you back," he added.

His reply humbled her. She thought of herself as quite giving and spiritual and yet here was a tattoo-filled, non-church-going individual telling her how to be kind to others.

Anna learned a lesson that day.

Whenever they were together, it was almost as if they wore a placard on their chests saying, "Hey we are here. Come ask us for money" as they always seemed to attract beggars. Even on the days they looked sweaty having just been from the gym or when they would dress down, it did not matter. They always attracted the poor.

Anna and Sonny were tied by their love for others in need.

There have been plenty of instances where they were dressed to the nines headed out to eat or watch a movie or see a comedy club, when they would pass or drive by someone who is stranded or appearing to need help, that Sonny would always stop and he and Anna would end up having to push a car or give aid to someone in need of food. It made them happy to help others and it brought them closer together.

They also both enjoyed working out or going for walks in the park.

## Bobby

The closer they became, the more Anna's resources got invested in Sonny's dreams. Sonny told her that the band's vision is to bring people together. Sonny was Cuban, Anna was Asian and Hispanic, Bobby was American. Two months of dating and he started calling her his wife. He knew about her failed marriages but was not hindered by it. To him, they were soul mates.

Anna later met Sonny's band mate Bobby. Bobby was very much into fashion. He didn't work and was very self-absorbed. Sonny told Anna that Bobby grew up in Los Angeles and that his dad used to know people in the music industry. When Anna asked why the band does not try to connect with the people that Bobby's father use to know, Sonny told Anna that Bobby's father did something terribly wrong that completely ruined all his ties to those people. Sonny wouldn't expound why or how.

Ann also later found out that Sonny was giving all the money he makes in bartending to pay for Bobby's apartment.

Bobby was unemployed when he met Sonny a few years ago. At that time, Bobby had not started singing yet. He was only the song writer for the band. They completed their video with someone else as the lead vocalist. Due to the difficulties that come with the journey to "making it", the previous band dismantled.

Sonny was the only one that stayed.

Bobby, being about thirteen years older than Sonny, brainwashed Sonny over the years that he, Bobby, was going to come up with the song that will make them someday be a hit. Ever since then, Sonny had always financially supported Bobby.

Having learned this fact, Anna thought of leaving. Every time she thought so, it seems she would accidentally come across Joel Osteen on TV and the message would almost always be about trusting and believing in God.

## The House

Sonny always sent Anna sweet pictures and text messages whenever Anna was at work. It was one of his ways of acknowledging that he knows and appreciates Anna's love and support for him chasing his dream.

One afternoon, as Anna was in her car driving home, she received a text of a picture of a beautiful house in California. Anna saw it and thought it looked like something worth several millions of dollars.

The jaded and angry-at-God part of her couldn't help but start talking out loud.

"Look at this fool! He sent me a picture saying this will be our house." Anna began ranting.

"I make more money than he does and even I know we can't ever afford a house like this," she continued.

Before Anna could utter another word, her thoughts were interrupted by a bible verse coming to mind.

Still alone in her car, she said out loud, "Hold up now. I'm driving. You know I have not been reading the bible and I don't ever memorize verses."

When she got to a stop light, she quickly searched for a pen and a piece of paper and wrote down the verse before she forgot. She quickly jotted 2 Samuel 7:11.

When she made it to their apartment, she flipped her shoes off, opened the one of the drawers where her bible had been hidden for months, though to her seemed like ages, and looked for the verse. Part of the verse said, "The Lord declares to you that the Lord himself will establish a house for you."

Anna was skeptical. Part of her said, "What are the odds of you talking out loud about a house and a verse coming to you that is pertinent to that which you are talking about?" The other part tried to dismiss it and said, "It's just a fluke."

Regardless of what it was, the loving part of Anna decided it was a sign meant for her to stay and keep supporting Sonny. They both have always thought they were each other's test. She was his test, if he stayed faithful to her and loved her despite of her bad "record" of failed relationships and he was her test, if she loved him while he had nothing. Anna passed the test.

## The Other Whoa-Man

In Anna's heart, there's no better joy than to eventually find herself loved by a man regardless of her previous failed marriages. They did tell her that the band was only a platform to show other men how to truly love women. She continued to find solace in the fact that she and Sonny always continued to do things for the homeless, whenever they were both off from work and can enjoy a day together.

Sonny and Bobby's relationship had eventually affected Anna and Sonny's relationship like a virus. Every time, Anna made any extra money for herself and Sonny, Sonny always used it to pay for Bobby's bills.

Bobby lived extravagant. He stayed in a high rise apartment, with concierge service, downtown. A place Anna basically pays for every month since Sonny always asks her for money and she knows no matter what Sonny says, ultimately it is for Bobby. Bobby went on dating sites as if he was some big shot. He would go on dates all on Sonny and Anna's money. But Anna knew how much Bobby meant to Sonny. He was after all, the one that changed it all for Sonny. At least, that is how Sonny explains it.

Sonny shared with Anna how he used to be fat . . . about 300 lbs fat. He told her how most women never paid him any attention or gave him a second look. But since joining Bobby's band, Bobby had taught him fashion and helped him eat healthy and eventually be the 190 lbs slim person that he is now. Sonny adds that Bobby would let him borrow some of Bobby's expensive Roberto Cavalli shirts.

During one of their fights, fueled by the continuous flow of Anna's income to Bobby's pocket, she told Sonny how all the money they have given Bobby has more than paid for the shirts that he once let Sonny borrow. Their fights are always because of Bobby asking money from Sonny and Sonny asking money from Anna.

The closer Bobby and Sonny got to finishing their music with the help of Anna's money and hard work, Bobby's evil ways became more apparent. He began telling Sonny that Anna needs to stop by at his place while Sonny is at work bartending so that Anna can help with brainstorming for the music video concepts. However, when Anna would go, on account of Sonny's pleading, it would be nothing but a "call to the principal's office" telling Anna that she needs to come up with more money and fully support the band because in Bobby's heart, he believes that Sonny is nothing without him. Bobby emphasized that if Anna truly loved Sonny, she should give her full support and not waiver at all. Sonny has always told Bobby about Anna's frequent attempts to leave since this is the very first time she literally had to live paycheck to paycheck.

**Father**

The pressure of having to upkeep Bobby's extravagant faux lifestyle, had cause friction between Anna and Sonny. It was pulling them farther and farther apart. One night, as Anna was alone in their apartment, she prostrated herself and cried out in prayer.

*Father . . .*

*I don't know where to even begin . . . all I know is that I feel very lost and alone. I know that I have no one but myself to blame for my circumstances. I made the choices and now must suffer its consequences. Was it really wrong for me to have always wanted a man who could love me as much as I could love, if not more? Was it wrong that even with the blessings You have given me I still always prayed and asked for more for my family and others? Should I just have been content with whatever I had when all this started? I don't know. What I do know is that no matter how despondent the situations I have been in the past, You always seemed to pull me through all of them.*

*I am once more in a situation as seemingly ill-fated as the ones I have been before. I cried out to You to bring me a man who loves me and loves to do good things for others and in my search ran into Sonny. At one point, I believed he is the answer You gave to me. At one point I felt loved, accepted and valued by him. However, lately it seems I feel I am more of a nuisance and "work" for him (as he puts it) more than anything else. How could it be that at one point I felt so lucky to have found him yet now feel like I am just another face, another step in his journey?*

*Though I will never regret that I gave my heart openly so soon, it does make me wonder if that is partly what kills the love—I mean his love for me . . . eventually? After all, he is a man and men love to hunt. Did I steal the joy of hunting from him by always being available and supportive? And because I have been hurt by others in the past, did I unconsciously always react negatively towards him? I remember feeling sure that he loves me but now I wake up every morning feeling like he is just being diplomatic. And because we both dislike anything that involves what we consider "drama", we seem to, for the time being, remain mum about our situation.*

*I do not have anyone to turn to but You Lord. My parents are far and even if they were close, they cannot do anything to help my situation. I do not have friends who think and love other people the same way I do. You are the only One who loves me despite my imperfections. Regardless of my iniquities, You can see what's inside of me. Even in the darkest places, there is nothing hidden from You.*

*Search my heart oh God. May you find my continuous desire for good things and blessings for even those who have wronged me pleasing and worthy of Your mercy. You have brought me here to this country and have made a promise to me. A promise of knowing Your plans for me—plans to prosper me and give me a future. And as unworthy as I may be or feel right now, I know that **You are faithful. Your love is not conditional. It is not bound by "if's, as long as, or because".** You love me and that is the end of it. I* *cannot do enough sins or enough mistakes to make You turn back on Your word.*

*Thank you God that You love me that much. Thank you that I can rely on Your faithfulness to see me through. Thank You that Your arms are not too short to reach out and rescue me. Thank you for the knowledge and assurance that my help always has and always will come from You. Thank you that Your timing is always perfect. You are never a minute too soon and never a minute late. Thank you for all the trials You allow my way. They are intended to polish the rough edges in me so that I could eventually be the best me You desire for me to be.*

*Keep me focused on Your greatness Lord. Keep me focused on what You are able to do and not on the magnitude of the problems I face for now.*

*I lift up to you all my patients and people I have met along the way and made a promise to help. May I live to see those promises come to fruition.*

*Lastly, I lift myself to You Lord. You know the desires that lie deep in the recesses of my heart—**the longing for unconditional love from another being**. Your ways are higher than my ways. For now, I only see the tangled "not-so-pretty" underside of the weaving but in due time, You will reveal Your plans for me. Use me Lord. Just like how You use the poor, outcasts and oppressed in the bible to convey Your message and shame the wise and powerful, do so with me. It would make a wonderful testimony and witness to the world if You would bless me—someone who has been thrice married, abused emotionally, physically and financially. Bless me with a love from a man who is*

*God-fearing, compassionate and a good steward of Your blessings. Thank you! In Jesus' name. I receive it.*

## Joel Osteen

It was two a.m. that day. Sonny and Anna decided to go to Publix. They both don't like being in the crowd.

As they stood in the self-service check isle, Anna felt a strong presence beside her. She turned to look and recognized a familiar face standing right beside her. She looked and saw who she thought it was. She took a second look and realized it was one of her favorite R and B singer. He was by himself. Because of her shock, she did not know whether to ask to take a picture with him or to just ignore him. Her timidity got the best of her and she chose the latter.

Little did she know that Sonny knew one of the music producers who worked with the said artist.

Sonny came home one day and told Anna that he told the producer to ask the artist to not to look at his woman.

"Love, (is what he called Anna) I received a text from the producer Tim asking me when the music will be ready," Sonny related to Anna with delight.

"Really?" Anna was in shock.

"Was he in town?" Anna questioned.

"He said he was working with who we ran into this week and I kidded that he was checking my woman out," he said with a chuckle.

"He sent me a text with saying that the artist was sorry but he couldn't help it as he thought you were one of the prettiest Asians he had seen," Sonny added.

"Haha. If that's the case, he must not go out much or maybe he needs his eyes checked," Anna humbly retorted.

"Tim saw your pictures and asked if you could send others," Sonny continued.

With Sonny's insistence, Anna did take some pictures to send to the producer. They were all taken in the gym at their apartment complex. Anna had no experience whatsoever in modeling. The photographer took three different pictures and even used the gym floor mat as a background. She wore the same outfit on all three pictures.

It has been about a week since Sonny has emailed the photos to the producer. Anna could not do anything but wait. The knowledge that the photos had been sent made her feel so embarrassed especially after she had research that when someone is asked to send photos or any modeling portfolio, people usually send about twelve to forty pictures of different looks, outfits and backgrounds.

One day, as she was by herself in the apartment, she sat in their white leather sofa thinking, "How stupid of me to even allow those photos to be sent? They were so amateurish. I am not the right size, the right height, plus anyone past thirty was too old for any modeling," she castigated herself.

As she started to feel down about the whole photo situation, she decided to turn the TV on to get her mind off of it and into something more positive.

Guess who came on? Joel Osteen.

As if he was talking to her, he said looking at the screen, "God is saying to you, I will give you back double for what the locusts have taken. You tell yourself you are not the right height, not the right shape, not the right nationality but I say to you, I will give you beauty for ashes. Others will see you how I want them to see you," Joel preached.

Running away from God, as she has done so in the past, she tried to quickly change the channel as she felt that certain recognizable warmth in her whole body and tears started welling up. "Rhema" is what came to mind. She remembers a college friend tell her that "rhema" is an utterance from God to the heart of the receiver. She quickly dismissed the thought and decided to get changed to go to the gym.

## Foolish and Weak

Anna has given everything Sonny asked—money to record, money to rehearse in the studio, money to edit, money to "master" the song, money to create shirts and wrist bands for advertising, money for video costume and production, money for lighting, the list goes on and on. She was feeling all the pain of sacrificing everything she had for someone else's dreams. She even agreed to the idea of speaking for the band's vision to women. Bobby had said he would like for her to tell other women of her failed marriages and her struggles. It was always something she dreaded. Not knowing what to do or where to go, being alone in the apartment, she lied down on the floor, and began to talk to God.

"Why did You even allow me to cross paths with these people (referring to Sonny and Bobby)?" Anna fussed.

"I don't have dreams of being in the spotlight. I have kept all my skeletons and past hurts locked and hidden in a closet and now they want me to share it with other women." She kept on.

"Who is going to want to listen to stories of failure and pain? And from someone like me? I don't talk, speak and dress the part." Before Anna could advance to more complaints, a verse came to mind . . . 1 Corinthians 1:27. Anna quickly grabbed her phone which sat on top of the leather couch beside her. In the search bar, she typed the verse. What popped up on the screen read,

". . . But God has chosen the foolish things of the world to confound the wise, and the weak things to shame the strong."

The surfeited Anna retorted back, "Oh so I am the foolish and the weak? Thank you for that vote of confidence! I love you too Lord!"

"I don't understand it Lord. Why do you keep allowing me to make mistakes after mistakes? Why don't You just show me where to go or which door to take? Matter of fact, don't even show me, just freaking shove my ass to the right door. I don't want free will. Just do it for me." Anna groveled.

"Please, I am tired, in Jesus' name. Amen," she concluded.

As she got up she and reflected back on how she talks to God, she felt grateful that God in His Mercy, had not sent a lightning bolt on her ass yet.

## Enough

It took so much before Anna decided to leave for good.

When, because of Anna's financial help, the band finally finished recording, Bobby got even more full of himself than he already was. Being that the record sounded good, due to so much money spent on editing and mixing and "doctoring" the music as Anna called it, Bobby saw himself more and more a god. Instead of just releasing the song as they had initially planned, Bobby wanted the music video to be more extravagant. The concept of the music video changed from how men should love women and became more and more about Bobby and his great fashion and what not.

Even though Sonny and Anna's love for one another was strong and everything she thought she wanted in a relationship, she did not like the relationship between Sonny and Bobby and how everything in their life is dependent on what Bobby said.

It wasn't until one day, when Anna's mother sent her money to help her with her financial situation and Sonny promised that the money would be used to finish the second song recording and release the song by You Tube but did not so and instead gave it to Bobby, that Anna finally took matter in her own hands.

## Matea

While Anna was at work, a co-worker asked her to see if she could talk to her. Her name was Matea. Their interaction had been limited to simple greetings of courtesy in the mornings when they would pass each other in the hallways.

Matea approached Anna one day and said,

"Please don't be offended but I saw you in my dream. God has asked me to tell you that someone in your family has breathing problems but that everything will be okay. God told me you have a beautiful heart."

No one in my family is sick, Anna said to herself. But remembering her days when she was what she considered a good Christian, she remembers learning that it is a grave sin to say "God said" if it was not really of God.

"Either this woman is telling me truth or she is up for time in hell for making things up," she thought. To test the woman's words, Anna texted her mother and asked if anyone in the family was having breathing problems. Anna's mother responded, "Why?"

Anna knew then that the woman was telling the truth. Before she could send another text, she received another message from her mother stating, "I. I am the one having breathing problems. I had just been diagnosed with congestive heart failure."

Anna thanked Matea for the message but still continued to wonder how the woman could have known about her mother's situation. Nevertheless, she felt relieved that the woman's last words were that "everything will be okay."

Weeks had passed with Anna still being with Sonny. Even though now they are living pay check to pay check and all her savings had been spent, she continued to believe in true love.

During the band's effort to get the music out, Anna even met a music producer whom she introduced to the band. He was willing to help the band produce their music but was very displeased with Bobby's arrogance, when he met him in person, that he ended up deciding not to help at all. The music producer told Anna, "Next time, don't even let Bobby talk at all. He is so full of himself. You will never get a record deal or have anyone agree to help until he learns some humility." Anna could not help but agree as the guy spoke the truth.

## Bobby's Selfish Ways

Since Bobby and Sonny wanted Anna to be the "face' of the band and to be the one to share her experiences with women from all walks of life, Sonny created social media accounts for Anna.

Anna was extremely opposed to this move as she was a very private person. The more the band wanted to involve her by assigning her as the "face" or making her the spokesperson, or including her in the music video, the more she wanted to leave.

The idea of being the spokesperson and having to tell others about her life scared the s—t out of her. For years, she had been successful in hiding from others her misfortunes especially in love and now these men (Bobby and Sonny) were expecting her to share them with others.

Weeks after the account had been opened, Anna received invites to be in music videos as an extra. Sonny also told Anna and Bobby that the producer had seen Anna's photos and was interested.

Bobby immediately called a meeting. He adamantly told Anna that she is not to respond and entertain any of the invites for modeling or music videos. He told her, "You are the face of the band. You cannot be in any music videos other than ours." He made the orders and Sonny and Anna always followed.

## Spiegel

Bobby was very manipulative. One day, through his brother Richie, he met a lady named Beth who had money. Beth wanted so badly to be a reality star. She was about forty five years old. Bobby sold her the idea that she would make a good TV host for a show that discussed topics that women dealt with on a day to day basis. Bobby showed Beth Anna's picture and told her that she, Anna and another woman, preferably of a different nationality, to cater to women from all walks of life and other countries, would make good

TV hosts. Beth got so excited and told her rich boyfriend Beardson about it. It would be like an international version of "The View", Bobby told Beth.

Beth was dating a rich man named Beardson who had a lot of connections and money to say the least. Bearson is the founder and president of a management consulting firm serving Fortune 1000 and brand-driven clients. He is also an author. Bobby had shown Anna's photo (without Anna's knowledge) to Beardson and Beardson was sold on the idea after seeing Anna's picture.

Beth was so caught up in Bobby's manipulative web that she had even invited Bobby, Sonny, Richie and Anna to Beardson's house while Beardson was out of town. Bobby, wanting to always look like the big shot that he is not, demanded that Sonny tell Anna to go with them and drive them in her Hummer.

Beardson's house was immaculate. It was in the same neighborhood were one of the famous rapper, lives. At least that's what Anna was told. The house had three stories and a basement which is a home theater. There were probably at least 8 massive bedrooms. There were big beautiful art pieces on the walls of the formal dining and formal living room areas. The curtains hung three stories high. Even the bathrooms had heated automatic and motion-sensitive commodes. The lid would sense the motion and moved up when someone got in front of it. The toilet seat temperature can also be adjusted. This guy has so much money he doesn't know how else he could waste it, Anna thought as Beth gave them a tour of the house.

"Look at this fool," Bobby commented to Sonny as he and Sonny looked at Beardson's wall pictures. "We are coming for your money you!" Bobby continued.

Anna saw the devil in Bobby's eyes that day. As Bobby toured the house, his heart filled with envy much like how Spiegel's evil side came out whenever he got close to the ring (from the movie Lord of the Rings). He also asked Sonny to bring several blunts with him as Bobby knew Beth likes to "smoke".

Before heading to meet with Beth at Beardson's house, Sonny had already warned Anna that Bobby and all of them (except Anna) would be smoking joints as "Bobby is trying to create a bond with Beth."

"I'm sorry love. I know you can't smoke with us because of your work and because you are really not into it but when we get rich, you won't ever have to worry about work," Sonny consoled her.

They drove in Anna's Hummer on Bobby's request. Bobby likes to appear like he's got it all. Beth was not aware that he has been unemployed for several years and has been financially dependent on Sonny and Anna.

They all smoked pot except Anna and were all eventually "high." The more high Bobby got, the more condescending his remarks regarding women became as they were watching reality TV shows. "Tell her the magic words I love you so you can get her in bed" Bobby yelled at the humongous flat TV screen as they watched. To Anna, it was a direct contradiction of what he initially told Anna their music was about—how to love and appreciate women. She thought of writing Beardson to warn him about Bobby's deceitfulness. She wanted to alert him how much money they had already taken from her and now that she is depleted, he is next. She feared he would not believe her.

Anna remained calm. As she saw the greed in Bobby's eyes, Anna told herself that night that she was going to end it all. She knew that without her financial help, Bobby and

Sonny did not have any credibility and would not have even gotten close to any semblance of the life they wanted to live. The little comforts and luxury they experienced were mainly due to Anna's good grace. To Anna, Bobby was nothing but a certified pimp. She was even able to come up with a song.

## Certified Pimp

### NOTHING BUT
### A CERTIFIED PIMP

**Five foot eight inches tall**

**He walks with so much balls.**
**With high-end fashion clothes**
**And click-clocking shoes,**
**He prances around for everyone to see.**

**Faux achievements on the wall,**
**Saying he has a higher call**
**Blind pimp-"ettes" on every corner**
**Hustles and slaves with his every order.**

**(Chorus:)**
**But I see who he is.**
**I know who he is.**
**He is nothing but, nothing but**
**Nothing but a certified pimp.**

**With every dime that's not his**
**He smugly acts and fakes bliss.**
**Like Judas and his traitorous kiss**
**His soul he didn't miss.**

No regret for every taking
So much pain others enduring,
But to him it has no meaning
Only matters is how much he's keeping.

(Repeat Chorus)

I fell in love with one o' his little pimp-ettes
As he, in pleasing him, does a pirouette.
True love gives and never takes.
Not this pimp's love though . . . for hearts it breaks.

So go on with your bad ass self you fool.
Your days are numbered if you think you're cool.
With one quick blink you will greatly sink
Because God above can simply break your link.

And I see you.
And I know you.
You are nothing but, nothing but
Nothing but a certified pimp.
That's all you'll ever be! Peace. (Throw money in his face)

Anna could only write in extreme emotions. She knew deep down how much she was beginning to abhor Bobby's conniving ways.

Even though Sonny had talent, his blindness to Bobby's deceitful ways has closed any opportunity for him to make it in the music industry. Bobby saw how much Sonny looked like a rock star and Bobby decided that he too would like to be one.

## The Warning

Anna went to work that Monday morning just like how she has done so in the past. As she was walking in, Matea was walking out. She did not realize that Matea's work schedule has changed. She went towards Matea mainly to greet her hello but as she did so, Matea proceeded with what she said was a word from the Holy Spirit.

"The Holy Spirit wanted me to let you know that some people are taking advantage of you. The money you have been giving is not being put into good use. The Holy Spirit is saying the name Sonny. The Holy Spirit asks that you leave the relationship that you are in now. If you don't, even your ability to help financially could be taken away from you in order to force you to leave and remove you from that relationship," Matea firmly stated. I also hear that you also need to get back to journaling your interaction with God," she added.

Anna was at a loss for words. Flashes of Bobby and Sonny smoking blunts using the money her mother had sent her came before her eyes. She didn't know how Matea could have known about her situation or even what Sonny's name was, when she and Matea had never spoken anything about it. In fact, her interactions with Matea were mostly exchanges of polite "good mornings" to one another. How could Matea have known that since meeting the band she used to keep journal of her dealings with God but that she stopped when her phone broke? She never spoke to anyone at work about her life. It could only have come from God. Anna did not even muster the guts to bid Matea goodbye. She just headed towards the building . . . . towards anything or anyplace that would take her farther away from Matea, her message and worst of all, God's wrath.

Anna remained preoccupied with the message from Matea all day. She couldn't believe that the man she thought was her soul mate was not the one God intended for her. She was beginning to doubt if God was even EVER with her. She felt her life always going in circles. Just as she would get close to anything she really wanted or really made her happy, something always happens and what she wants or what she finds happiness in vanishes in thin air.

Anna worried that if she did not leave Sonny, God will take her work—her ability to make money, away from her and it would gravely affect her family. They have always depended on her. She always sent them money for all of their expenses. Broken hearted, Anna began to write her last words for Sonnyy as tears fell from her eyes like they were never going to end. The letter was as follows . . . . .

*My dearest Sonny,*

*I write this letter with tears running down my cheeks. I have been through a lot in my life but deciding to leave you is the hardest by far. You said we are soul mates.*

*When we first went out and I saw your compassion towards the poor, I thought I found my match. I felt so blessed, so happy, so energized, so hopeful that I slowly desired to return to God.*

*But I don't know what happened. Somehow, somewhere, you changed. You were no longer the humble, kind, and loving person I thought you were. You started becoming full of yourself, deceitful and manipulative. Through it all, I still loved you.*

*I am not perfect myself either but I know that the love I have for you no one can match, not in this lifetime. I loved you for you—you without money, without any means of transportation, without any good credit, without a nice body, just you and your essence and love for the poor. That is the reason why I stayed for as long as I did.*

*I know that if not for Bobby's influence, you would have been humble enough to accept this truth—You are nothing without God but you have allowed someone to brainwash you and misguide you. You've even allowed him to destroy your relationship with your parents.*

*I wish I could hate you but it is not and will never be my nature. I want you happy and blessed with or without me.*

She could not believe it. Sonny came in her life when she was not even looking for it. It almost even seemed to her that he started making her believe in God once again. Sonny was just like her . . . very compassionate to the poor. They both loved fashion and very rarely fought unless of course Bobby had asked for money. Sonny's dreams have awakened Anna of a dream that she never thought she had. Anna realized how much she wanted to help the poor on a much larger scale. She did not know how she was going to do it. Sonny's dreams, if realized, could help her realize hers she concluded.

But her dreams were being shattered right before her very eyes. She questioned where God had been all along. She was angry and resentful that she even crossed paths with Sonny and his band mate. She did not see the purpose of why she had to go through with what she went through or was still going through. If there was any lesson to learn, she has not learned it, is what she thought.

## Death of a Dream

Matea knew from the way Anna left her this morning that she did not take her message well. She worried she might have hurt Anna badly. She called to check on Anna.

When she heard Anna say hello from the other end of the line, Matea began reassuring her.

"Are you okay? Be strong okay? I know it's not what you want to hear but I have to tell you what the Holy Spirit is telling me to say."

"You have to leave. God will be with you but first to have to obey." She advised.

"This is not right! I did not ask to be here. I met them and every time I tried to leave before, it seemed God told me to stay. Now, all of a sudden He tells you to tell me to leave? He can't even tell me himself? What of the times when verses would come to me that I don't even know of and it would always be pertinent to what I was talking to Him about?" Anna answered with indignation as she was weeping.

"It must just be you trying to preach to me!" Anna accused.

"I can only tell you what I am led by the Holy Spirit to say. I'm so sorry. Be strong and obey," Matea comforted.

"I gotta go. I can't take anymore of this!" Anna hung up.

She fell on her knees by the bed. Alone in the room she stretched herself on the floor and wailed as if someone has died. She wept all night until she couldn't cry no more and she fell asleep.

## The Get Away

The night that she left Sonny was a night she will never forget. Sonny had been sensing Anna's desire to leave. Anna had asked Angelina to help her pack her clothes and shoes as quickly as possible while Sonny was at work. She has attempted leaving Sonny in the past but her love for him has always made her stay. Sonny had no idea that he would later find her gone. He even called Anna and left her a voicemail saying I love you an hour before she completed packing and loading everything that she wanted to take on Angelina's truck. But based on how Sonny had used her, she questioned the sincerity of his "I love you" voicemail. She left him all the furniture, appliances, every thing that she bought. Anna had asked to moved in with Angelina at least until she could find an apartment.

Anna had planned weeks in advance how she was going to get the vehicle back that she has allowed Sonny to use since she has been helping the band. When she had asked him for it days before leaving, Sonny acted as if it was his. She knew that trying to be mature and civil and talking it out did not work as her leaving meant the end of financial backing for the band.

Anna had never visited the place where Sonny worked. When she decided she was going to get her vehicle back, she used Google earth to locate where the place where he worked was. Google earth even showed her where her vehicle was parked. Thanks to technology.

He asked Angelina for a ride. Using Garmin, she found the place, waited until no one was in the parking lot and then quickly got out of Angelina's car and inserted her spare key into the ignition of the jeep she had let Sonny use. Anna droved off and felt like she was in some movie's action scene. She did it. She got her jeep back.

## The Falling Out

Anna and Angelina were like sisters. Whenever, Anna would go shopping to buy something for herself, she always ended buying one for Angelina as well. In the two years of their friendship, they have loved and opened themselves to one another like most blood sisters do. Anna even met Angelina's family.

It was only to be expected that Anna could find shelter in Angelina's house, when she needed a hide away from her "get-away".

Anna stayed at Angelina and her husband Marlon's house for about three weeks.

Angelina loved to go out. Even on the days that she went out with others, Angelina always used Anna as her excuse. Every weekend or night that Angelina was out, her husband always thought she was with Anna not knowing that Anna only went out with his wife but once a month. Angelina was not happy at the fact that having Anna in her house might mean less opportunities for her go out at night.

Anna had met Angelina's husband even before her "stay" with them. She found him weird and "off".

One day, when Angelina was out with one of her lovers, she had asked Anna to keep her husband busy so he would not notice.

Anna never really liked going out on week nights so she agreed and decided to stay in the house. She was too tired from work anyway.

As she and Angelina's husband were watching TV, he told her something that shocked her.

"I have something to show you," he confessed.

"What is it?" Anna asked.

He showed him a picture of her on his phone.

"What the f—k are you doing with my picture on your phone?" Anna angrily questioned. Ever since her abusive experience with her ex-husband, she was done with goody-goody Anna. Even though she has noticed that back then it seemed her connection with God was like 4g Pentium processing in speed, she didn't care or want to care anymore.

Anna recognized the picture and knew she had not sent it to him and it was not any picture that he might have just cropped from her pictures with Angelina.

"I have always been attracted to you," he continued.

"I show the picture to men at work and tell them you are my friend," he added.

"You are sick! You know I am friends with your wife. Why would you do that?"

"Things have not been well with she and I for years now. I have always noticed how very loving and supportive you were to your husband Miguel, how hard working and ambitious you are and I think we would be a good match," he went on.

Anna could not believe what she was hearing. She went to Angelina's place to find temporary peace from the mess she just left with the band. Yet, here she is again, trapped in bullshit. She must be once huge crap magnet she thought.

She did not tell Angelina what happened. She just decided that she needed to find a place of her own as soon as possible no matter the cost. It was getting more and more uncomfortable for her to be at the house knowing he was "eyeing" her.

When Anna needed help with her vehicle, Angelina's husband volunteered to help. Anna tried to be as respectful as possible to her friend Angelina and her husband. Unfortunately, the more polite she was, the more Marlon thought he had a chance with her.

One night, as she was in the guest bedroom where she stayed while at Angelina's house, she received a text from Angelina's husband.

"I had hired a private investigator and I know she had been seeing other men," the text read.

"What are you talking about?" Anna pretended not to know anything.

"I know she has been doing things. She is only with me for the money and the green card." he kept on.

"Please leave me alone. She would be furious if she even found out about you texting me. How did you even get my number?' she asked.

"I took it down and saved it on my phone when I accompanied you to get some work done on your vehicle. I figured you would not just give it to me if I asked," he admitted.

"You are crazy!" she said exasperated. "I will never be with you! You are crazy! Crazy!" Anna reiterated.

In the days that passed, Anna tried to bury herself with work so that it would be almost sleep time by the time she got home. She made it obvious to Marlon that she was not interested.

On Anna's third week at Angelina's house, Angelina's brother had arrived from their country Guatemala. Angelina and Marlon recently started a pressure washing company and had a contract that would pay them $60,000 once completed. Marlon and Angelina brought Angelina's brother to pay him to work "under the table".

But Angelina's brother has sticky hands. On the day that Anna moved her stuff out of Angelina's house, she left her phone in the guest bedroom and went to the bathroom for a brief moment, that is, less than five minutes and her phone was gone by the time she returned to the room. It was only Anna, Angelina and her brother in the house.

Anna knew Angelina would never steal her phone so the only person left that would was Angelina's brother. For fear of Angelina's brother discovering Marlon's texts to Anna, she decided to tell Angelina the truth about Marlon's attempts to get with her. Little did Anna realize that when she made it obvious to Marlon that she was not interested and that she was soon moving out, Marlon had covered his ass and told Angelina that it was Anna who had told him of Angelina's "escapades". Angelina always envied Anna's income. Now it was her chance to make big money and nothing and no one is going to stop it. Angelina believed Marlon's lies. She lost her friend.

Angelina chose to believe Marlon, her husband. She has to. Her green card depended on it. And the "all-American dream" depended on the green card. They never spoke again.

## The Screen Saver

Anna, Sonny and Bobby were into the power of visualization. WHEN, in the beginning, they were still very committed to pure intentions of creating music that uplifted women, Anna had saved a picture of all three of them and set it as her home screen saver after they shot the video to the first song that they recorded and had copyrighted.

In the weeks that followed after they had committed to creating music that uplifted women, Anna had seen initially, how everything was falling into place. Though highly opposed to social media being that Anna was a very private person, she allowed Sonny to create social media accounts mainly for the band but with Anna as the face. Anna was able to get a response back from Anthony Hamilton, and Demi Lovato. She was also getting followers. She was always doubtful if they were real or fake accounts of the said celebrities. She always wondered at the odds that she would have the REAL account of any celebrity being that she had very little knowledge about social media.

Anna even asked her self, "Who are these followers? Why are they following? Where are we going?"

After all that transpired in her life recently with Sonny and with Angelina, Anna deleted her current screen saver and changed it to a picture of God carrying a woman in her arms as she said, "I'm soooo tired Lord. Carry me."

# Chapter 7

## Through the fire

Nothing came easy for Anna. She always had to work hard for whatever she had. She felt that no matter how giving she was, everyone that she encountered seem to just take advantage of her. She has read motivational books to keep her focused despite the many ups and downs in her life. She read in "The Complete Works of Florence Scovel Shinn that " . . . every man is a chain in the link of my good." This night, however, she could not convince herself that it was so. Her mind was filled with memories of people who took advantage of her.

### Janel

During the time she decided to stop going to church after her most physically abusive ex-husband Tommy, Anna ventured into flipping houses to keep her self busy.

With her good credit, she would find houses on foreclosure and spend a little money to improve them and then sell them for a profit. She learned to paint walls like a professional. She learned to caulk, put moldings, lay tiles, check roof shingles, stage furniture, etc.

The house she had with Tommy, she kept. It was a big 4 bedroom, two-story ceiling high, 2 ½ bathroom with Jacuzzi, beautiful house. She couldn't part with it even with the bad memories from her wife-beating ex-husband. Not until she met Janel Whitley.

She met Janel through one of her co-workers. Janel, during one of their interactions, had mentioned to her how she wanted to own a beautiful house but could not do so because of her bad credit. Janel is a single mom of two boys.

One day, Anna invited Janel and her kids to her house. Janel and the kids loved her house. Janel has heard that Anna had other houses. She asked Anna if she could stay and rent the house for a year and later purchase the house from Anna once her credit improved.

Anna, being the sucker for sob stories, quickly came to the rescue. She figured she could turn the house with painful memories as something beautiful for someone else so she agreed. Janel was so thankful.

"You are a blessing!," she told Anna.

Within a month, Janel and her kids moved into Anna's fully furnished house.

Around the fourth month, Janel started having money problems. Almost on a monthly basis, she was either late or she was short of a couple hundred bucks with her payments to Anna. Feeling bad for Janel, Anna did not make it a big deal. Since the mortgage was in her name, she paid it on time every month regardless of how much or how late Janel's payments were. She believed Janel was doing the best that she can as a single mother of two. Anna's big heart has always been her strength and her weakness.

On the twelfth month of Janel's stay, she had told Anna earlier during the month that she would soon be interested in purchasing the house and transferring the mortgage in her name. By the end of the month, Anna received a voicemail from Janel telling her where she left the keys to Anna's house. Confused by the voicemail, Anna drove to the house to speak and clarify things with Janel in person.

Anna was hurtfully surprised that not only had Janel and her kids left, she also took all the furniture and brand new appliances from the house with her. Anna was sick to her stomach but she did not want to deal with the issue and did not like confronting devious individuals. She decided not to file a police report and just take everything as a loss and move on.

## Shana

As Anna tried to suppress the painful memories from her past of individuals and situations which were each racing to come up to her conscious brain first, she decided to drink wine to numb her feelings.

Unfortunately, the wine did not help. It only made her more emotional. Flashbacks of her co-worker Shana came vividly to mind.

Shana was from India. She had long black hair. She was fairly smart but very arrogant and condescending of others. She also was always very envious of Anna. Shana likes being told she is the prettiest, smartest and best looking in the group.

When patients could not remember Anna's name and describes her as " the very pretty girl with long hair", Shana fumes with jealousy.

Shana also despised the fact that Anna was big on customer service. Anna was polite to family members and visitors. Whenever Shana would see Anna helping a family member, co-worker, or visitor, especially if it happens to be a decent looking man, she would always give Anna a hard time.

"Ooooohhhh who's your new boyfriend Anna?" she would kid.

"I saw you talking to that person," she would add.

Shana was a bully. Every other co-worker followed or always agreed with her even when they know Shana is being mean to others.

Anna would just smile, shake her head and walk away. She did not believe in wasting her saliva on stupid trivial things. Even though Anna would so love to give Shana a piece of her mind—a knuckle sand which on her face for that matter, she did not do so. Anna tried her best to sweep it under the rug, Shana's comments gradually left their mark on her. Anna soon stopped looking good for her self. When getting ready for work, she started not ironing her clothes and not combing her hair and just put it up in a bun so she would not get more remarks from Shana. Anna figured, "let her think she is the best. So what? I know who I am."

That kept things quiet. The less pretty and smart Anna appeared, the calmer Shana was. Despite Anna's attempts to run away from God, deep down inside she knows she still has a connection with Him. Anna tells herself and sometimes even others, since she has not been going to church and not been praying like she use to, that her reception with God is a little static-ky since she is not like how good and nice she used to be. Anna would even kid that her "line" with God is so poor that she gets frequent drop calls.

Although there is a big part of her that wants to stay close to God, all her previous painful experiences remind her constantly not to do so. Anna felt burned.

## Lamalia

Lamalia was Anna's boss in one of the places where Anna had worked. Lamalia was single and a few years younger than Anna. Lamalia was kind in the beginning to Anna. But there was no other way she could be towards her. Anna was her most reliable, most productive and most respectful staff.

However, due to Shana's influence and gossipy nature, Lamalia's treatment of Anna soon changed. Even knowing that Anna was her most productive, most efficient, most customer-oriented and most knowledgeable staff, Lamalia soon started treating Anna with disrespect after giving in to Shana's prodding.

Shana filled Lamalia's brain with so much lies that Lamalia could no longer see straight. All Lamalia thought was that Anna was out to get her position. Lamalia's superiors liked Anna and Anna used to be a manager and now Anna wants her job, are the thoughts that ran in Lamalia's head.

Regardless of the fact that Anna has told Lamalia repeatedly that she was not interested in a management position, Lamalia was convinced Anna was out to get to get her.

"Anna, please write this appeal and work on this denial," Lamalia tells Anna.

"I don't know this patient. I did not work with him." Anna politely replied.

"I don't care. Work on it." Lamalia ordered knowing that Anna was her smartest most capable staff. Lamalia also knew Anna was kind. The bully in Lamalia's inner being told her she could treat Anna that way.

One day, while Anna was writing up one of her reports, a bible verse popped in her head. Psalm 23: 5-6.

Anna had been running away from God for a while and thought that she was in the clear.

The "good" side of her still recognized God. She said without words, " Hold up now Lord. You know I have not been reading the bible. Let me Google this up."

Anna got her smart phone from her pocket and Googled the verse. The verse said, "You prepare a table for me in the presence of my enemies. You anoint my head with oil, my cup runneth over . . ."

Anna laughed as she read the verse. She doesn't want to believe in God anymore.

She sarcastically found herself muttering, "God, I think You might be wrong. Are you sure this message is for me? You must be overworked. I know there are some women who don't like me and are envious of me, but I don't believe I have enemies," she internally retorted. She dismissed the thought and went on with her reports.

Three weeks later, some commotion arose. Some he-said she-said situation came up and Anna heard her name dropped in the middle of it all.

Anna heard the still small voice inside her say, "Remember when I told you that you had enemies?"

Anna was stunned.

Anna tried to get back to work but she heard the still small voice say, "Turn in your resignation."

Anna was in shock. So much in shock that instead of an internal dialogue she heard herself say out loud,

"Whaaaat? This is crazy! Who resigns because a still small voice told them to? How would that look in my resume? Reason for leaving previous job? Uhh . . . . a still small voice told her to?"

"I can lose my license and be looked at as crazy for this?" Anna continued.

Anna was always herself when it came to God.

When Anna did curse or use the word "f—k" and she knew she did, she would tell God how "f—k" was only an adjective or an adverb to describe what she was feeling at the time. Anna figured she cannot lie to God since He knows everything so she might as well admit it. Besides, Anna was making every effort not to be good. She knew that godly people received more testing and she did not want more of it.

"What am I going to do? I have not been looking for another job nor have I been going for interviews. You know my family depends on me," Anna's rebuttal.

"Turn in your resignation now!" is what Anna heard inside.


Much to her own contradiction, Anna turned in the resignation the next day. Her boss Lamalia accepted and appeared happy to get rid of her. She was after all "the" competition.

Lamalia's bosses heard about the news and soon requested a staff meeting with everyone with lunch paid for by them, the "higher-ups".

As Anna listened, along with her peers, to the "higher-ups" request to come to "them" before deciding to leave the company, one of Anna's co-workers remarked,

"You know this meeting is about you right? They don't want you to leave."

Anna headed home after work. She later received a text message from her boss Lamalia asking if she would reconsider staying. Lamalia would even offer to match what offers Anna was getting from other companies.

Anna, at a loss, since she had not planned on resigning to begin with, decided to ask the still small voice.

"Does this mean I should stay since they are willing to offer me more to stay," Anna inquired.

"No. This happened so that you will know that what I say will happen happened," she heard the small voice say.

The jaded and running-away-from-God part of Anna argued, "Ugh! but this place is so much closer to my house!"

Anna's contention fell into deaf ears.

## Euince and Michael

Anna continued to drink wine.

"You even turned water to wine remember?" Anna was beginning to be inebriated. "Why is it bad if I drink then?" Anna argued to her ethereal friend.

The more she drank, however, the clearer her memories of past hurts became. Her painful experiences which she has buried deep down inside her were all bubbling up to clear consciousness.

Eunice and Michael was a couple. Eunice use to work with Anna in one of the places she has worked at. Anna always thought that Eunice was a nice lady. Eunice later introduced Anna to her husband.

They had been decent acquaintances. One day, Eunice and Michael borrowed $700 from Anna and Anna felt that she could trust them to pay her back. They said they needed it for some emergency and that they would pay her back right away. They did.

About four months later, they borrowed again. This time, they borrowed seven thousand. They told Anna that they are in great financial distress. The Pisces in Anna, who always wants to "save the day", gave in. She let them borrow. She later realized that they did not intend to borrow. They intended to take. They changed their phone numbers and never answered when Anna called and never came to the door when Anna rang the doorbell of their house. That's another one for you gullible Anna, she told herself.

Anna did not take them to small claims court as she believed it would just take her time away from work. Anna learned from one of her favorite books "The Millionaire Mind" that we all have blueprints. She has learned that it there is one thing she knows well, she knows how to start from scratch, work hard and save money again. So she did.

## Sophia

As Anna continued to drink hoping to make her self pass out, the more emotional she got. She recalled other events that have happened to her.

Sophia is someone she met when she was still with Tommy. Sophia was going through an abusive relationship as well, that's how she and Sophia became close. Sophia is a Colombian lady married to Tommy's friend. He too was abusive just like Tommy.

When Anna's divorce with Tommy was finalized, Sophia had asked Anna for them to be roommates since Sophia was also going through divorce. Sophia had only been in the US for 2 years and does not have any credit history. Anna agreed to help and allowed Sophia's name to be on the lease, the power and utility bills. They shared the expenses, though not equally. Anna paid two thirds of the monthly bills and Sophia paid one third. Sophia only worked as a housekeeper so she could not afford half of the rent. Anna likes helping others. It somehow always reminded her of where she came from. She did not want to ever forget that she was from a poor family.

They stayed for a year together. They went grocery shopping together, went for night outs together, watched tele-nobelas together and cooked and ate together.

Their self-esteem is the only thing they did not have in common. Even though Anna was two years older than Sophia, Anna was 27 and Sophia 25 and Anna was 10 lbs heavier than Sophia, Anna was always very confident. This quality always made her more attractive to men.

"I don't know why when we go out, the owners of the restaurants or the managers always seem to like you. If not them, you always manage to meet doctors and I always end up with the bust boys or waiters," Sophia complained.

"I don't know. You are sexier and prettier. Look at you with your abs all out," Anna complimented Sophia as Sophia loved wearing blouses that showed her abs.

"Ugh! Sometimes you make me mad," Sophia blurted.

Anna has never taken Sophia's words seriously. She figured Sophia is younger and she just has to let her be. Sophia is always craving attention. Anna remembers that there is one guy Sophia was so crazy about. His name is Stephen.

Sophia was so crazy about Stephen that even when Stephen tells Sophia that he has a girlfriend that he is in love with, Sophia still agrees to be intimate with him. Anna started disliking the fact that Stephen was almost always in their apartment locked in the bedroom with Sophia.

Little did Anna know that the times that Stephen has walked past her ever so briefly in the apartment, he has noticed her. Anna was always doing something productive—painting, sewing, scrapbooking, etc. Anna did not know that Stephen or anyone noticed.

One afternoon, while Anna was on the floor doing some arts and crafts, Sophia comes home obviously annoyed over something.

"What's the matter?" Anna asked out of concern.

"Nothing" Sophia quickly responded.

"It's something. What is it?" Anna insisted.

"It's Stephen. He irritates me. Every time I ask him to go somewhere, he always says sure. Then he adds why I don't invite "Anna" to go with us," Sophia explained.

"I think he likes you. No I take it back. I KNOW he likes you," Sophia angrily added.

"You like him don't you?" Sophia accused Anna out of sheer insecurity.

"No I don't! The only reason why he even gets to be inside this apartment is because I know how madly and crazy in love with him you are!" Anna snapped. She has been quiet for several months now and allowed Sophia to do whatever she wanted including bring any guy home that she liked whatever time of the day Sophia pleased. Anna was strongly opposed to different men coming in and out of their apartment. She did not want their neighbors to think bad of them.

When their lease was up, Anna moved out. She did not want to wait until things got really bad between them. She has helped Sophia already build her credit for a year and that was enough.

## The Family

As if she wasn't already feeling enough misery, she also remembered all the things that she has done for her family that they do not seem to appreciate—the house she paid for, the two cars she bought them and the money that she sends on a regular basis. Anna sends at least $7-10,000 a year to her family but they always seem to complain about not having money.

She recalled years ago, when she went home for a 3 wk vacation to her country. She tried to buy her parents a silver Honda sedan. She sent the initial $15,000 for her mother to buy the car so that by the time she came home a week after sending the money, her parents could give her a ride. When she finally made it home a week after sending the money, Anna did not find a new car in her parents' house.

"Where's the car you bought ma?" Anna inquired.

"There is no car" her mother dryly responded.

"Why? What happened?" asked Anna.

"I was on my way home after exchanging the money at the black market instead of the bank because I was told the black market gave a better exchange rate."

"After I had exchanged the money and was on my way to the bus, some guy snatched my bag from me and quickly disappeared. There was nothing I could do." Her mother explained as if trying to make an excuse.

Anna's heart sank. She had saved that money for them. She avoided shopping or purchasing anything for herself unless if was a need and not a want. She slept in a sleeping bag for two years and did not buy any other furniture other than a radio. Now she's being told that the money went "poof", gone, and is now nowhere to be found.

Anna wanted badly to make her parents happy on their 25$^{th}$ wedding anniversary so she wire transferred another $18,000 and purchased her parents a car. It was their first car ever. Anna delighted in seeing her parents happy. They were getting old and commuting and running after jeeps and buses was beginning to be very difficult for them.

Anna tried to enjoy the rest of her vacation with her family but never received an apology for them having lost the money she had previously sent.

## The Purses

Four years later, Anna decided to come home again. She misses the food, the places, the family. Anna has been able to save more. Her sister Dong also now has a daughter of her own. Anna wanted to surprise her sister with $2000 to open a savings account for she and her daughter. With the exchange rate of fifty pesos to a dollar at that time, Anna's sister would have 100,000 pesos in the bank.

Anna flew economy. She wanted to save her money so she could give more to her family. She also bought purses for her sister. They were of all different brands—Baby Phat, Liz Claiborne, Jessica Simpson. When she finally got home, she could not wait to show them to her sister. She wanted to make her smile.

The next day she motioned her sister to come with her in the bedroom. She gestured for her sister to sit on the floor with her as she began to open her luggage. She showed her the purses saying,

"I got these for you."

"Baby Phat? Liz Claiborne? Who are they?" Dong grumbled.

"Why you didn't get me Louis Vuitton or Dolce and Gabanna purses?" Dong continued to fuss.

"Sorry, I didn't know. I thought these were good since they are more expensive than what I would even get for myself," Anna apologized.

She was saddened by her sister's reaction. She had a different picture in her mind of how her gifts would be received. She was hoping to see a big smile or even get a hug. She was totally caught off guard.

## BOSE Speakers

Anna took a couple of days to adjust to the time change then proceeded to help her parents prepare for the Christmas reunion that was to be held that year at their house. They all went to a Misa de Gallo (mass during Christmas eve), a tradition in their country. The next day jeeps loading kids, women and men, all of which were Anna's relatives arrived. Anna's parents prepared so much food. They had menudo, apritada, spaghetti, pansit, kare-kare, lechon, fish relleno, seafood including lobsters, king crabs and oysters. They also served cases and cases of beer for the men and games with prizes for the kids. They also rented a giant Karaoke machine. Anna's family loves karaoke.

After the reunion was over and all the cleaning had been completed, Anna presented her sister with the gift—$2,000 cash. Her sister thanked her and went to sleep. Anna was very tired and several hours later went to sleep as well.

Around 11 o'clock of the next day, Anna was woken up by loud music. She heard "Dame mas gasolina" by Pitbull and could feel the vibration from the base from whatever speakers they were coming from.

Anna finds her sister in the front porch listening to the music. Anna saw brand new speakers. They were black and had the easily recognizable logo of Bose speakers.

"Are these new?" Anna asked.

"Uh-huh!" Dong replied.

"From who?" Anna prodded.

"You! Who else?" Anna's sister answered smugly.

"Huh?" Anna clarified. "What do you mean?"

"From the money you gave me yesterday. Duuuh!" Dong stressed.

Anna was shocked. She knows what Bose speakers cost being that she's owned them in the past. She could not believe, however, that her sister chose to use almost half of the money she gave her to buy Bose speakers and listen to reggaeton instead of putting in into savings for her and her daughter's future. Anna was sad and disappointed. She was also angered by her sister's selfish decision. Anna hates confrontation and arguments so she didn't say a word. She waited until it was time for her to leave. Anna has never been back home since then.

## Contempt

The more pain the memories brought, the more Anna drank. She knows she's not supposed to but she rationalized it with the fact that she's hurt. She also began projecting her pain to her ethereal "friend".

"You don't love me," she began. "I hate this heart You've given me. Others just keep taking advantage of me," she continued.

"I have done nothing but tried to be good to others all the time and yet look what it got me . . . . biiiiigggg fat nothing!" She was drunk.

"Where did it bring me?" she continued.

"In f—ing nowhere!" she emphasized.

"It seems everyone just always wants to take from me," she grumbled.

"Oh yeah? . . . what about the parable of the prodigal son? How crazy is that? The older one does all the good, the younger one fucks up then decides to come back and what does he get? Wooohooo! Best robe, ring, sandals, fattened calf and a party??? Really?," Anna kept on.

"That's what I will try to be. I want to just be bad. That way you will welcome me. I want a robe, ring and party as well." She had been crying as she was drinking. Anna was not sure if it was her swollen eyes or the alcohol level in her system that made those words her last statement before she passed out and fell into deep sleep.

# Chapter 8

## Her Miracles

Anna woke up the following day only with a desire to drink again. She was longing how close she seemed to be with God way back when she first became a Christian that she always came boldly before God. She was like a kid. Whenever she asked and prayed, she never waivered. She just believed and waited. She had Pentium 4g processor when it came to God. Now it seems when she calls on Him, she gets drop calls.

She began drinking but this time, memories of God's goodness surfaced.

### Black Outs

Anna was assigned the task of washing the family's week long dirty clothes every Saturday and the task of ironing everything, from uniforms to work clothes for the coming week, every Sunday. As such, she had very limited time to study. She was then still in college.

She remembers one Sunday she was ironing clothes, She has a final exam in school the following day and did not feel ready at all for the exam. As she ironed, she kept thinking, "Hurry up Anna! If you finish by 6 pm, you can still have at least four to five hours to study before you have to go to sleep."

Usually around six in the afternoon it starts to get dark. She thought she was doing well with her time management.

Around 5:30 p.m. she only had one or two more pieces to iron before she could rest and begin studying.

Around 5:45 p.m. as she was on the last piece of clothing beginning to be happy, the electricity went out. They call it "Black outs." She could not believe it. It was already beginning to get dark. It was very difficult for her to study with just tiny candles on.

As a new Christian, she wanted to practice whatever little she knew about the bible. She had read miracles in the New Testament from the book of Acts.

She locked the door, knelt down on cold cemented floor, closed her eyes and began to pray,

"dear God. I need to study but just as I completed my chores, now the electricity went out. It's hard to read in the dark using just itty bitty candles." Anna explained.

"Your Word says that Your power is not bound by space nor time. It even said something about Your arms not being short. Electricity would not be a problem for You then. I will know that it is You who answered my prayer if the electricity comes back on at exactly six o'clock p.m. It is now 5: 47." She informed God.

"I need it to be at six o'clock okay? Not a minute late and not a minute soon. In Jesus' name I pray, Amen." Anna said boldly.

Anna got up and unlocked the door. She began lighting up candles so she could find her way around the house. Her mother was asleep in the other bedroom. Anna decided not to worry. She did not even begin reading or studying. She figured she would wait until the lights were back on. She was calm at first. The last two minutes before six, seemed like hours. As she saw it was already 5:58 p.m., she wondered if she should have started reading already. She felt a slight fear for having wasted time. She quickly dismissed the thought and tried feeling happy and anticipating the light coming on just as she had asked. At 5:59 p.m. as she sat in the sofa alone in the living room, she said out loud, "You have one minute Lord." She waited. As the red colored second hand of the clock hit the number 12 to mark the time at exactly six o'clock, the lights flickered and the electricity came back on.

"Hallelujah!" Anna screamed as she stood up from the sofa.

The noise woke her mother up and she asked Anna what the noise was about.

Knowing that her mother got mad when she found out that she had been attending a different church, she pretended and said, "Oh nothing. I was just happy that the electricity was back on." It was the first time she said hallelujah.

## Parole Visa

It has been about a year since she left her country. She received a letter from her sister. She was ecstatic. The letter read:

Dear Anna,

I miss you. I have nobody here to tell me what not to do. I have been skipping and cutting classes and started doing marijuana. I have no one to compare my body against to know if I am getting fat. (Her sister Dong always use to call her "baboy" in their language, meaning pig, as she always thought Anna was a lot heavier). Hope all is well with you. Miss you.

Anna's heart dropped. That was the first time, her sister had been affectionate and said "miss you" to her. Anna's sister also sent pictures taken while she was goofing around making faces while high. Anna cried. She decided she needed to go home to visit and help her sister out.

As she wasn't sure of the procedure, one of her friends told her that it was not a good idea to leave the country since she had just applied for adjustment of status. She was told she had to have a parole visa which usually takes 6 months. Six months is too long, Anna thought.

Before buying a ticket, Anna prayed. "Lord, I need to see my sister. She is not well. I was told that I need to have my parole visa before I could leave or I would not be able to come back. I don't have one. I cannot wait six months. I am going to buy a ticket for next month because the ticket will be more expensive the closer it is towards December. A lot of people come home during Christmas time and the plane tickets go up," she explained as she always does. Anna made the phone call and bought a ticket.

Three weeks had passed and still no visa. Three days before her scheduled flight and still none. Anna thought it would be best to remind God. "Lord, three weeks had passed. We bought a plane ticket together remember? If You don't send my parole visa, I will forfeit my fare and if they do refund my money, it will not be the full amount. You wouldn't want that would You? Please send my visa so I can go. In Jesus' name, Amen."

Anna continued to believe. Her parole visa came in the mail the day before her flight. Though she didn't have much time to pack, she was very grateful. She had no doubt, God worked to make it happen.

## Her Mother's Promotion

Back when she was still in the Philippines waiting for all her papers to clear so she can move to the U.S, her mother was up for promotion as principal. There were other candidates up for the position who had more seniority and more experience than her mom. Anna knew how important it was to her mom so she went and hid in her room to pray.

Anna prostrated herself and began to speak. She has been reading the bible a little more everyday and was trying to incorporate her learning as best as she could. As such, her prayers were fluctuating between reverence and just talking normal to God.

"Lord, I thank You for Your goodness. I thank You for Your mercy. You have been good to me. My mother is about to take an exam to get a promotion. There are other candidates for the position. My mother is not the "sharpest tool in the shed." But You can make her. Please show her favor as you have shown me. Help her with her exam and give her favor during her interview. Let her taste and see Your kindness. In Jesus' name, Amen."

Anna's mother goes through the exam and interview and tells Anna and the rest of the family later that week that she made principal. Anna said quietly, "Praise God."

# Chapter 9

## A Whole New World

### Be Still

Anna was always generous and kind-hearted. One thing she is NOT, is patient.

Anna loves being married. Despite being very career-oriented, she is not one to say "I don't need a man." Anna always saw woman and man as the completion of God. To her, woman represented the "compassionate" side of God and man the "just" side of God.

It is her love of marriage that has made her make mistakes after mistakes in the past. Anna loves the thought of having someone to come home to, someone to share her dreams and thoughts with, some one to enjoy and experience life with.

As she went from one mistake to the next, she has come to realize that she was part of the problem. Even though in the beginning she believed that God is able, somehow Anna later started only coming to God when it came to her finances. With matters of the heart, even when she would ask for signs, when she doesn't get them, she takes over and tells God to not worry about her love life as she will handle it.

"Handled it you did, NOT!" Anna kidded herself.

"You could have had your own scholarship program named 'Anna's-Take-advantage-of-me' foundation with as much money you have spent on failed love and paying for ex-husbands' student loans and debts," she further denigrated.

She, at one point, even tried to blame it on her parents being strict and not allowing her to date until after she completed college that has caused her to be very naïve with matters of the heart. She also figured that it was the reason that made her say yes to a marriage proposal from the first boyfriend she ever had. Then she accepted another proposal from the second boyfriend. That's really smart Anna, she tells herself. She just won't be still and allow God to do the work.

Every divorce left Anna starting all over again both financially and emotionally. To her, getting up and dusting herself off was getting harder and harder.

## Joshua

Even before she met Miguel she knew a guy named Joshua. They met when she used to take Salsa groups lessons when she and Sophia lived together. He is from Honduras and was about five years younger. They began dating briefly but Joshua traveled internationally for a living. He told her he does something with private acquisitions. He tried to explain it to her one day and it just went over her head. He is usually gone about three months at a time. Every time Joshua would leave the country to work, by the time he gets back, Anna has already found herself a new date or boyfriend.

When Anna told Joshua that she has married Miguel because he always leaves her, Joshua continued to stay in touch with Anna as friends. They always got along. Anna could not think of one incident when she and Joshua had a fight or disagreement back when they were dating. Anna recalls all their interaction to always be pleasant and exciting. It always seems like there's never enough time. In the past, Joshua always asked Anna to meet him wherever he was—China, Japan, Thailand, but Anna could never just quickly drop work and travel with him. It seemed they could never make their schedules work and have time enough to really know one another.

After her get away from Sonny, Anna re-communicated with Joshua via text. She and Joshua have known each other for over seven years now.

Whenever Anna would get drunk and miss Joshua for being out of the country working, she would often times tell Joshua to just leave her alone.

"Tu no me amas," she texts him.

Joshua, being the non confrontational guy that he has always been just ignores her texts and changes the subject.

"Que tal babe?" he asks.

They dated for a good five months (if staying in contact via text counted as dating). Most of their interaction was mainly through texts.

Anna, being the person that she is, always craves the actual physical company of a man in her life. Ever since the fall off her friendship with Angelina, all the more she wishes Joshua was in town.

## Bert

It was not long after Joshua had left until Anna decided to give an old ex-boyfriend another chance. It had been five months since she has not seen Joshua.

His name is Bert. He was a sales person who works only 2-3 hours a day. What a life, Anna says. Even though he often told Anna to go shopping and use his credit card, Anna could not do it. She was never the type of woman who hustled men for money. In fact, in her case, it seems it was always the other way around. She was the one always hustled by the men she loved.

Bert is very fun-loving and generous. He also likes to joke around and make Anna laugh. Since he usually goes home early after working 2-3 hrs a day, he developed a very bad habit. He is an alcoholic. Although he refuses to admit it to Anna, Anna knows that seeing a new empty bottle of vodka every week is a good indication that Bert has more problems than what he cares to admit.

Anna decided to bravely ask Bert questions one day.

"Why do you drink so much?" Anna inquired

"I don't drink a lot!" Bert disputed.

"Sure you do. I see a new empty bottle of vodka almost every week," Anna contended.

"I don't do anything bad. So what if I drink a lot?" Bert retorted.

Anna didn't respond. She knew he had been drinking. She, based on past experiences, knows all too well that it is just a matter of time before they get into an argument. That's how it has been since they got back together. He was fun and loving until he got above .05% blood alcohol level. After that, he gets argumentative and demeaning. They fight almost every three to four days. His frustration over the fact that he wants to already be married to Anna also surfaces on a consistent basis especially when he is drunk.

He has been asking her to move in since they started dating again. Anna still remembering all the pain of her previous marriages, could not find the guts to say yes. Though financially enticing to her as she would no longer have to pay about a thousand five hundred dollars to keep her own apartment and other monthly bills, she declined his offer.

She remembers him telling her during one of his "drunk" moments that he started drinking more when he found out that she got married immediately after they broke up seven years ago. Memories of the fun times he has had when he went to visit Anna's country remains fresh to both of them as if it was just yesterday.

## The Trip

It happened seven years ago. They met and soon started dating exclusively. Christmas of that year, Bert asked if he could travel with her to her country . . . Anna's country. He was doing well at work that time and insisted that they go business class. That is exactly what they did. Even though Bert drank considerably during their travel and their trip, she did not see it other than the fact that he was on vacation and deserves to have fun.

It was late at night when Anna's parents picked both of them up from the airport. They were happy to see her. They were also surprised to see a 6'4' man towering over them. They were always fascinated by the Americans. Their country was a naval base at one point and housed many G.I Joes. Because it doesn't happen frequently that they are in the company of an American, they could not stop staring at him.

When they finally got to Anna's parents' house, they showed them their bedroom. It was a twin size bed. Both Anna and Bert were too tired to even complain that the bed was too small. Anna and Bert slept on their side. That was the only way, they can both fit in the bed. Anna also warned Bert that out of respect, there was to be no hanky-panky in her parent's house

Days later, it was Christmas day. It is a big day for Anna's family. It was reunion day. Bert was amazed to see a professional size karaoke machine rented. He was also shocked to see several vehicles unload what seemed like a never-ending unloading of relatives. Some of which Anna had not seen in years.

Bert remembers having hoards of relatives arriving all throughout that day. He and Anna had given Anna's parents money to help with the food expenses. They had a never-ending supply of beer as well as plates and plates of food for everyone. They also had games for all the kids—singing contest, newspaper dance, scavenger hunt etc. Prizes included 100 pesos or what was equal to $4 at the time. It was all a blast.

Bert, having grown in an orphanage, did not really know what it is to be with the family. All that he learned was that it was fun to be in her country. He stood out in the crowd. Since most men from Anna's country were 5 feet tall, Bert towered over most of them. Bert also had an advantage during basketball. There, in her country, he felt loved and appreciated.

After weeks of fun with Anna's family, Bert and Anna returned to the US. They returned to reality, that is.

## Christine

Weeks after their return from their trip, Anna got to meet one of Bert's closest friend. His name was D. He is fake, Anna thought. She remembers how D loves hanging out with Bert because Bert always paid for everything. D also "borrowed" (meaning never to pay back) money from Bert to pay for his girlfriend's boobs. Furthermore, D loved it whenever Bert was intoxicated. That is always when Bert is the most vulnerable. When he is high or when he is drunk.

Anna remembers all four of them going to dinner one night years ago. Bert had already been drinking at his house before they even got to the restaurant. When they sat down and shared the table with Christine and D, they all soon ordered afterwards. Bert's lobster came first. He was already drunk. He cut a piece of the lobster meat and instead of asking Anna to try, he stabbed it with his fork and offered it to Christine.

"Try this. It's really good," Bert said.

Christine opened her mouth wide and took what Bert was giving. After which she said in delight as she licked her lips seductively while gazing at Bert,

"Ummmm . . . . that;s really good!"

She is a big flirt, Anna thought to herself. Anna started drinking to forget about the incident and later got too intoxicated. Anna's emotions welled up.

"You like her and you want her," Anna told Bert.

Bert was already beginning to sober up this time and as such felt judgmental enough to tell Anna she was 'tripping."

Bert did not know how to comfort Anna. He retreated to what he knew well . . . . he pretended she was the problem.

Days later, Anna decided to end it all and their communication terminated.

## Take Two

Going back to the present, feeling alone without Joshua, Anna allowed Bert in her life again. It was their second go-round with their relationship.

Bert was relieved to learn that Anna was "available" again.

Bert had repeatedly asked Anna to move in with him but Anna would not budge. There was something about him that did not sit right with Anna. He was extremely controlling. He wanted to know which gym she would go to, how long the class was, what time she was leaving work, so on and so forth. Anna only really wanted to have someone to do productive things with—go to parks, try different restaurants, exercise etc, so she won't be tempted to go out at nights. Even though, he was normally funny and loving, whenever he got drunk, Anna recalls him being very controlling and accusatory.

"Ooooohhh, who's calling you on your phone?" he begins asking Anna when he gets drunk. Even if all it was a text from her boss telling her something about work. He gets paranoid and assumes she's been sleeping around based on the fact that she did not want to move in with him even though he offered to take care of her. Anna remembers one of their arguments.

"You have someone else! I tell you I am in love with you and I want to marry you but you won't agree to move in with me," he starts yelling drunk.

Anna was done with being bossed around or yelled at in relationships. Bert has also been drunk around her several times before and has embarrassed her in public and mainly when they are out in restaurants. The minute Bert started yelling, she yelled back.

"You're a piece of shit!" Anna counters.

"I tell you I'm okay with you drinking but not to be drunk every day every time!"

She added.

Bert being drunk sarcastically responded, "Well what kind of shit am I? Am I like dog shit . . . . like little mice shit . . . Dove shit?" he eggs her on.

"No! You are like smelly diarrhea, oozing in your paints, hurting-your-stomach, kind of shit!" Anna fired.

Bert was speechless, then they both busted out laughing.

Bert always admired Anna's fierceness.

## PRO-found

Anna always had difficulty letting men take care of her. Could it be that her years of having to always take care of others robbed her of the ability to allow others to do good to her even though deep down inside that is what she longs for, someone to love her unconditionally, someone to take care of her? She asked herself.

Anna was continuing her path to running away from God. She continued to curse, drink more on the weekends, even tried smoking cigarettes. Every now and then Bert sees the "good old" Anna he fell in love with in the very beginning. He knew that she was smart and fun but very God-fearing.

Whenever he was sober, he would record Joel Osteen for Anna seeing how his teachings always puts a smile on Anna's face and the gentle and loving spirit back in her.

One Saturday morning, Anna came to Bert's house to help clean up his place. She had not seen Bert in days and she knows he starts drinking heavily again when she is not with him. She knew he had been drinking heavily the night before. She found bottles of vodka, cigarette butts, dishes piled up in the sink. She saw him unkempt and still in wearing the same jumpsuit he wore three days ago.

She helped him walk to the bathroom and asked him to shower and clean himself. Anna walked back to the kitchen to begin cleaning.

Anna heard Bert yelling, "Beh beh . . . (baby), Beh beh . . . ."

"I just had a moment of enlightenment," he continued yelling.

She ignored him and continued cleaning.

Bert soon came out of the shower butt naked and walked staggering towards Anna to the kitchen.

"You know, I just had a very profound thought while I was in the shower!"

"You know how to spell profound?" he asked Anna.

Anna trying to patronize Bert replied, "No. tell me, how it is spelled?"

"It's P,R,O, found. Profound!" he spelled assuredly.

Anna kept herself from laughing as Bert looked quite serious as he continued to require her full attention.

"You know how all the other women that I have been with wanted to have kids with me and I didn't want to? You're the only one I want to have a kid with even though you don't want to," he proceeded.

"Well God gave everyone their own piece of clay. He told them do what they want with their clay. They cannot copy from others or look at what the others are doing. Well guess what?" he asked Anna.

"What?" she replied calmly hoping this conversation would soon be over.

"I am your clay. Do what you want to do with me," he stated with a childish smile on his face.

"Uhumn . . . . .that is profound alright," Anna sarcastically agreed.

As Bert turned to head to the bedroom to get dressed, Anna returned back to cleaning and said to her self, "This fool gets a moment of clarity while completely drunk! That is so strange."

## Prelude

Bert constantly bugs Anna to move in with him. Even though, Anna though it might be financially beneficial for both of them, Anna feared it was not worth all the emotional and mental stress that came with it.

From her previous experiences, she has learned that she allows men to enter into her life and gives them her trust because she just needed a warm body and was never patient enough to wait on God. And that is what exactly she got—a warm body. Oh and yes, pain and suffering to go with it. And their cousins—shame and fear.

Anna realized she was doing the same thing again. She saw a preview of what life will be with Bert. One day she got off work early, called Bert to make plans to meet him for dinner and rushed to her apartment to get changed.

"Hey you okay?" she asked Bert when he picked up after she dialed his number.

"Yup." He replied.

"Dinner together? Can you pick me up around 7 pm? I need to shower." Anna informed Bert,

"Sure."

"See ya in a bit," Anna concluded.

Anna's cell phone rang. It was Bert telling her he was waiting downstairs. Anna had not given Bert a key to her place because there was something in him that she could not trust. Anna despises that Bert gets very vindictive and accusatory when drunk. She told him she's headed downstairs.

When Anna came to meet him in his black Mercedes, he came out of his car and with his arms open wide said, "Don't I look handsome? Got the T shirt you got me, the fancy watch you picked, my cool-looking jeans and the Versace cologne you got me."

"Yes you do," Anna agreed.

She knew he was drunk. She felt annoyed as she had asked him before if he was drunk and he said no. Had she known he was drunk, she would not have made plans to go out with him that night, yet here he is now to take her somewhere.

Anna said, "Let me drive since you had been drinking." He gave her the keys and walked to the passenger seat.

As she was driving, Bert was trying to touch and kiss Anna. She could already see in her head how he was going to be when they get to the restaurant as this was not the first time he has been drunk before. She was getting even more annoyed. She doesn't like him "acting a fool" in public. At least, not when she is with him.

She told him to stop trying to touch and kiss her. Bert snapped.

"What's wrong with you?" he yelled.

"That was a big mistake you fool!" said Anna internally. "Not only have you lied that you were not drunk but that now I am having to drive you and now, you have the audacity to yell and ask me what is wrong with me?" She continued in her head.

Anna changed direction and headed back to her place. Bert yelled again.

"You are not going back in or else . . ." he warned.

"Oh no, he didn't just threaten me," Anna answered back internally.

She tried to keep her cool and they made it to her floor's parking deck. She handed him his keys.

Bert, furious and acting out, quickly grabbed her phone.

"Oh you're not going with me? Let's see who you'll call and go out with tonight," he accused.

"Bert, stop! Please hand me my phone back," Anna pleaded.

"Oh no!" teased Bert.

As Anna tried to grab her phone from Bert she dropped her keys.

Bert, upset that Anna snatched her phone back from him, quickly got to the driver's side and hid Anna's keys behind him.

As Anna was trying to pry open his hand, Bert started yelling to get other people's attention so Anna would just agree with him. "These are my keys. You are trying to take my keys."

"That's it you a—hole!" Anna whispered to herself. Bert's action triggered her switch from zero to sixty. She detested public fights or argument scenes between couples. She always found it trashy and uneducated.

Her previous training in self-defense kicked in despite Bert's 6'4" stature. She was able to get his keys from his hands and ran to her other car, a jeep wrangler, parked a few spaces away from Bert's car. She locked her self in and Bert kept banging on the car window and would not leave.

"Oh my God! Please help me!" It was déjà-vu all over again of her second fall.

Anna entered 911 but did not hit the "call" button. She showed it to Bert while still locked inside her vehicle.

Having had a previous DUI (driving under influence) record, Bert hesitantly walked away and got in his car. He harassed her all night with texts telling her how mean she was to him. She ignored the texts. Days later, she accepted his apologies yet again.

## Infinite Intelligence

Though not wanting to have anything to do with church or with God anymore, Anna still craves the power of speaking positive words in one's life. She has read the Complete Works of Florence Scovel Shinn and tried to apply it in her life. Instead of allowing fear in her life, she would use some of the affirmations she has read from the book. She loves, "In the Divine Design, there is no limitation, only health, wealth, love and perfect self-expression."

It filled her need for a greater being without the fear of having to go back to church and go through trials and testing.

## Mechanical Repair

Anna always likes to put her learning to application. She had been reading a lot about visualization, metaphysics and the power of spoken word. She was learning that everything had a frequency and emitted vibrations. She craved being positive but did not want it to have anything to do with the Supreme Being that is in the bible. She learned something about the Divine Mind. It appealed to her since it seemed more scientific than spiritual in nature.

When her car needed repair and the cost totaled almost $3,000, Anna remembered that she had signed up for some kind of mechanical repair insurance that would reimburse her for any repair done to her car provided she submitted the receipts and detail of why it was necessary. When she phoned the number to the company, she was told that she should have obtained approval first prior to initiating the repair on the car. The lady that she spoke to seemed understanding and told her to write a letter explaining why she did not follow procedure and obtain prior approval to begin with. The lady warned Anna that most of the time, claims without prior approval are denied.

Anna decided to put her learning to test. Prior to faxing the paperwork and letter explaining why she failed to obtain approval, she spoke the words, "There is no loss in the Divine Mind, therefore, I cannot lose anything that is rightfully mine."

She faxed the paper and prepared her mind to receive.

Anna did receive a check of reimbursement from the company. The universe is beginning to align and give her favor. She was beginning to be happy and optimistic with everything. Even when she is faced with challenges, it does not seem to faze her as much anymore. She quickly reminds herself that the adverse situation is " . . . only a link in the chain of her good."

## Waxing

Though it has been years since Anna has been inside a church, she still wonders why, run as she may, God still finds a way to communicate to her. Yeah, she agrees, her communication lines are not as clear as they used to. She wondered if she truly had a relationship with God at one point or even now. It seemed that when she speaks to other Christians about the Lord telling her to do something, she gets an odd look like she came from Mars. She remembers telling a co-worker about how God will often lead her to give money to a complete stranger and when she obeys, the stranger would tell her of how the stranger had been needing the financial help or had been praying for it. The co-worker, whom she thought was definitely more spiritual and pious than her, told Anna that she has never experienced hearing from God. Anna felt alone and lost. She was beginning to convince herself that maybe she is only imagining things or maybe she just dreams things.

It wasn't until one day, when she went for her usual waxing, that she would soon find herself in the company of people much like herself.

"Ohhh . . . that hurts!" she complained then tried to cover her mouth to keep herself from screaming.

"It's almost over," her friend Lou comforted.

Her friend tried to engage her into conversation to get her mind off of the pain.

"What are you doing this Thanksgiving?"

"Bert and I are going to help with Hosea feed the hungry. His friends invite us for dinner but I wanted to do something for others," Anna replied.

"Oh that's nice. My boss does something similar," Lou commented.

"My boss said that sometimes she hears God tell her to bring food to a certain place and she would drive and drive and stop wherever God leads her to."

"That's nice," Anna remarked. At least someone else hears God and she does not seem crazy, Anna said internally to herself.

Before long, the waxing was over and they bid each other goodbye.

## A Message of Hope

One night, while Anna was in her apartment, lying in bed reading a book on her Samsung Note, her thoughts were interrupted by a verse. Jeremiah 24:6-7. She wanted to ignore it but felt a curiosity to see what the verse was about.

She got her tablet out and typed the verse on the search bar as she has done so in the past. The verse read, *"My eyes will watch over them for their good, and I will bring them back to this land. I will build them up and not tear them down; I will plant them and not uproot them. I will give them a heart to know Me, that I am the Lord. They will be my people and I will be their God for they will return to me with all their heart."*

Almost in rebellion feeling that the message was for her, Anna in her heart answered God, "How do You propose to do that? I ain't going back to church?" Anna didn't wait for an answer and went back to what she was previously reading.

## Let Down

It was the week of Thanksgiving that year. Weeks prior, Bert asked Anna what she wanted to do for thanksgiving. Though they were invited by Bert's friend Laura to have dinner at their house, Anna told Bert she wants to do something different. She wanted to do something for the hungry. Bert complied. He told Anna he was going to sign them up with Hosea feed the hungry. Anna was so excited.

The weekend before that Thanksgiving, Bert went with his boss to New Orleans to gamble. They had planned and booked it way before Bert and Anna got back together. Bert promised to drink and gamble with control (as if there was such a thing) and to be back in town to go with Anna for her citizenship fingerprinting. He also promised that they would feed the hungry, as planned, for Thanksgiving.

While in New Orleans, Bert had texted and called Anna several times. Although she could tell he had been drinking, he seemed still somewhat in control. He is a functioning alcoholic, Anna told her self. Bert told Anna that his friend had asked him to go to a strip club and he declined and opted to sleep the alcohol out of his system back at the hotel. Bert also told Anna that he was up by one grand.

Anna, not wanting to be pessimistic, supported Bert during every call. She even kidded, "If you are up a grand, remember what Kenny Rogers' song says . . . know when to walk away." She didn't want to be like a mom to him. She just told him to be safe and have fun.

Tuesday when Bert was supposed to accompany Anna, he didn't make it. He was so drunk from the night before and was in no shape to drive with Anna to immigration. He lied and said the flight was delayed as the reason for why he didn't make it. Anna tried to be understanding and didn't make a big deal out of it.

The day before Thanksgiving, Bert tells Anna by the phone that he didn't want to feed the hungry.

"Hell to the f—king no! Why should I wash dishes?" he answered still drunk.

"But you said we will," Anna fussed realizing he let her down three times this past weekend. He lost the money he won, he didn't make it with her to her citizenship appointment and he didn't sign them up to help feed the hungry as he had promised.

Anna hung up the phone and called her friend Lou if she could join her instead. Anna remembers Lou mentioning something about feeding the hungry at church. Anna, even though running away from God, still loves doing good for others. Only problem is when she is faced with adversity and gets drunk, she gets mad at God and tells Him of all the good things she has done that she feels God has taken for granted.

## Melt Down

Anna's friend Lou, texted her the address. She offered to meet Anna in the school in front of the church as she said the church is slightly hard to find.

Anna, practicing her affirmations prior to leaving her apartment, told herself, "Infinite Intelligence I give thanks that I will arrive at the church without any difficulty."

Anna wore something comfortable. She put on a black long sleeved top, distressed jeans and knee high boots. She figured she needed to be able to stay up on her feet in case she was assigned the task of dishwashing or serving food. Her friend also told Anna that most of the church members speak Portuguese.

"That's okay," Anna thought. She figured they can still gesture to her what they need her to do.

Finding places is not one of Anna's forte. Even with her trusty Garmin, she has been lost in the past. Anna was shocked that she found the church without any problems even though it is somewhat hard to find.

It was a very small church. It read, "Freedom Ministries." Anna got there early and decided to just go in and text Lou to just meet her inside the church.

As Anna walked in, a very welcoming gentleman in a suit came up to greet her. He introduced himself as Pastor Dave. He led Anna to a small office, right of where Anna was standing, and introduced his wife to Anna.

"Hi! My name is Anna." Anna extended her hand to the lady.

"I am Daria. I am Portuguese. You speak Spanish?" the pastor's wife asked.

"A little," Anna responded.

"Where are you from?" the pastor asked.

"I am from the Philippines." She answered.

"Then you won't have any trouble understanding me during the service," he assured Anna.

Eager to start helping, Anna continued, "I am a friend of Lou. I told her I wanted to help feed the hungry so she invited me here. Tell me what you need me to do so I can get started. You can assign me to wash dishes or anything you want."

"Oh don't worry. There's nothing much to do. We all bring food and after the service, we all eat together. You see, the Brazilians don't have Thanksgiving so this is something we do for them," he kindly explained to Anna.

The couple explained that most of the church goers speak Portuguese and only about 15% are Americans.

Daria and Dave brought Anna to the main room of the church. Anna was the first few to arrive. She saw about three people on stage rehearsing the praise and worship songs, she saw a few staff in the back of the church checking lights, sound and arranging the chairs. Daria led Anna to the church kitchen on Anna's insistence.

Daria introduced her to ladies who were getting the tables set-up. Anna recalls their names as Rose and Lucy. They were very welcoming as well. Daria brought out boxes of plastic utensils and asked Anna to place then in the utensil holders.

"What an easy job," Anna said to herself as she stood in the kitchen counter arranging the utensils.

Anna was always trying to learn in whatever situation she was in. As she was arranging the plastic utensils which took no more than five minutes, she tried to read the sign by the sink written in Portuguese to see if she can understand.

The writing appeared as " . . . ajudar a manter nossa cassa limpa e organizada"

Anna speaking to her self very slowly as she was attempting to understand the writing,

" help maintain our house clean and organized,"she guessed.

Since there was nothing else to do, she sat in one of the church seat and waited for her friend.

She watched people as they arrive. Anna always enjoyed people watching. She always thought there is so much that one can learn from other's body language. Though most of the people that came in spoke Portuguese, it appeared everyone was very warm and welcoming. They all mostly greeted with hugs instead of the formal hand shakes. Everyone seemed like family. There were children running around, ladies talking and catching up with one another but all in all everyone seemed friendly.

The more she looked around, the more she realized, it was a church service. They weren't feeding the hungry. They were all sharing food and eating together after the service.

As she sat by there by herself waiting, she couldn't help but talk to God.

Anna's internal conversation was, "Did you just trick me? Did you purposely use the language barrier to make me misunderstand what Lou said and think that we were actually feeding the hungry?" She thought she wasn't ready to return to God. It wasn't what she came for.

When her friend finally arrived, she introduced Anna to her beautiful kids, Nadia and Thalia. She noticed her friend was wearing a church dress. As she looked around again, she realized, so did most of the other ladies.

"Crap! It is a church service." Anna said to herself. She didn't want to be rude so she decided she was just going to stay until the service was over. More people came including Lou's boss and her mother. Anna couldn't remember everyone's names.

Daria walked to the front of the room and began speaking in Portuguese. The interpreter translated in English. The worship music played softly in the background as Daria spoke. Though she heard mostly Daria's voice and couldn't hear much of the translation, she felt a familiar feeling. It reminded her of the warmth of the presence of God.

She started to feel different emotions she has suppressed for years—pain, resentment, anger, the wanting to run towards God, the peace from worshipping, the shame and desire to keep running away. The music kept playing with the worship team singing, "O Ele me ama . . . ele me amou (which she would later learn to mean He loves me . . . he loved me)." Before long, tears were streaming down her face.

"I must just be close to my period. This is just hormones," she was telling herself.

She had fought hard over the years not to let God back in her life, not to let herself want to get close to Him again.

It went on for about fifteen minutes. She found some tissue to wipe her face as she did not want to call anybody's attention to her tears. The praise and worship concluded, and she felt relieved. She figured it must be her hormones and the background music playing ever so softly is what is making her cry.

Pastor Dave opened the sermon with a bible verse—Ezekiel 36:26. The verse came up on the big screen by the pulpit. It read, "I will give you a new heart and put a new spirit in you; I will remove from you your heart of stone and give you a heart of flesh."

Anna began to weep. She knew then that God was talking to her. She had been fighting for years the urge to return to God. Out of the over thirty one hundred thousand verses there are in the bible, what are the odds that the pastor would have chosen this verse if not of God. As she bowed her head and closed her eyes to pray, Anna asked for forgiveness.

"You found me Lord. I have been running. Forgive me for everything I have done. I have made a terrible mess of my life. I cannot undo it but You can take charge of it from here on out. I am tired of doing it my way and failing over and over. I failed miserably Lord. Thank you for loving me even when I don't deserve it".

Anna, though grateful to be at church, couldn't wait for the service to be over so she could hurry home and have quiet time with God with her whole being down on the floor in reverence to God. She was still crying even as she got in her Hummer to head back home. This time they were tears of joy. It has been a long time coming.

# Chapter 10

## Epilogue

Anna lives today blessed and happily doing what she loves—caring for the homeless. That fateful Thanksgiving day was used by God to mark the beginning of a new chapter in Anna's life. She is also surrounding her self with her new God-given family to help her get and keep her life on track with God. She knew she would not be able to do it alone.

Everything made sense. The universe (created by the One, The Almighty Living God) did conspire to reveal to Anna her Divine Destiny. Anna made mistakes after mistakes looking for true love. She tried to cover acts of disobedience to God by doing good deeds and empty sacrifices.

Little did she know,  that the nudges from the still small voice to begin writing about her life and experiences was because God was writing the ending to her disobedient prodigal self  of seven years and beginning a new work (her year of jubilee)  to complete His promise of permanent provision to her.

## THE NAME CHANGE

In the Bible are many instances of when God has changed an individual's name. They were done to mark that God has caused a life change that would make them entirely different people.

Anna was not always Anna. It began a month before Anna began writing this book. She started writing just for her own personal journal and intended it to be about her quest for Prince Charming.

She met one of her neighbors during one ordinary day. They shared and talked about each other's normal everyday lives. They soon became friends.

One day, as Sebastian was talking to Anna, he told Anna how he was planning to buy another car. Anna, at the time, they met and became friends, had two cars. He always alluded to Anna as being very lucky. He told her casually, "I am going to buy a car and keep the one that I have now. I am gonna pull an Anna."

She corrected him in frustration. "How long have you known me yet you cannot remember my name. It is not Anna," she stressed.

Sebastian replied, "I have been known to call people by who they REALLY are."

Later that night, as Anna (who was not yet Anna at that time) questioned herself.

"Do I look like an Anna?" she wondered. The name Anna always seemed too plain and unappealing to her.

She looked up the meaning of the name Anna. She found that Anna is the Latin form of the Hebrew name Hannah meaning "favor" or "grace."

A voice told her, "This will be your name."

"Hahaha! Oh yeah? I am highly favored alright judging by the way my life has been pretty shitty," she sarcastically retorted.

Little did she know that it will truly be God's new name for her.

"Just Anna? No last name?" she teased.

"Legaspi," she heard the still small voice.

"My maiden name?" she asked.

"You couldn't come up with any other name?" she refuted sarcastically.

She didn't get an answer. Curious, she googled the meaning of Legaspi and found that it was a variant of Gavriel which means "God has given me strength." Anna was dumbfounded and did not understand why a name is needed.

"The story is about My unfailing love and not about you," she heard the still small voice.

## THE RESIGNATION

In Chapter 7 of this book, Anna shared the incident about her resignation. Anna used to be a very obedient Christian when she first began. Although her prayers were not always holy-sounding, they were very powerful. She was able to move the hand of God.

If you have read the book in its entirety, you know full well how much Anna kept running away from God much like Jonah in the bible did. As such, she went from hardship to another hardship.

Her resignation, followed by her get-away, were the two consecutive times, ever since her self-imposed willful disobedience to God, that she obeyed even though it did not make sense and did not want to do so. God uprooted her from where she was at and began planting her in a new soil.

Now, as Anna continues to live, she realizes that it was when she obeyed that God began the works to slowly return her back in His loving arms. Anna had lost all her savings during her struggles. But her obedience to turning in her resignation and leaving the relationship, restored her back to God's favor. God placed her in a job that offered her a better pay and afforded her opportunities for overtime. God has already began restoring her finances and will be true to his promise of giving her back double for what the locusts have eaten just like He has shown Anna when she first learned about tithing.

Though Anna continued to be good to others even when she had stopped going to church and was running away BUT it was not what God wanted. She was making mere sacrifices by trying to do good when God demanded obedience not sacrifice. (1Samuel 15:22)

## ANNA'S DESIRE

Even when Anna was at her worst behavior, she always had a big heart. Carrie Underwood's song "Change" could not have said Anna's desires any better. The song goes,

*What you're gonna do with the 36 cents sticky with coke*
*on your floorboard*
*When a woman on the street is huddled in the cold*
*On a sidewalk bench trying to keep warm*
*Do you call her over, hand her the change.*
*Ask her a story, ask her her name*
*Or do you tell yourself*

*You're just a fool, just a fool to believe you can change*
*the world*
*You're just a fool, just a fool to believe you can change*
*the world*

*What you're gonna do when you're watching TV*
*And an add comes on, yeah, you know the kind*
*Flashing up pictures of a child in need*
*For a dime a day, you could save a life*
*Do you call the number, reach out a hand*
*Or do you change the channel, call it a scam*
*Or do you tell yourself*

*You're just a fool to believe you can change the world*
*Don't listen to them when they say*
*You're just a fool, just a fool to believe you can change*
*the world*
*Oh the smallest thing can make all the difference*
*Love is alive, don't listen to them when they say*
*You're just a fool to believe you can change the world*

*The world's so big, it can break your heart*
*And you just want to help, not sure where to start*
*So you close your eyes*
*And send a prayer into the dark*

It is Anna's heart's desire to touch lives even if it is one at a time.

## LANGUAGE OF LOVE

God knew that the years of running away had turned Anna's heart into a heart of stone. God also knew that if He called her using any of the languages she spoke and understood—Tagalog, Spanish, English, she still would have ran even farther away.

God used the unspoken language of love—actions not words. Using the Portuguese people who were in the church that day, Anna saw acts of kindness, compassion, love for family and community, humility and reverence to God. All of which, familiar to her what seems like eons ago, she saw and felt as she looked around her within the small unassuming church. Little did she know that God has allowed certain difficulties in her life for a reason.

When God called Anna back in His arms, God used the pastor to cause the topic to be about "grace"or "favor", the name God told her will be her name. God also used a language she could not speak—Portuguese.

*Deus sabia que os anos de fugir se transformou o coracao de Anna em um coracao de pedra. Deus tambem sabia que, se ele a chamou usando qualquer uma das linguagens que ela falou e compreendido—(Tagalog, Spanish, English), ela iria corer ainda mais longe.*

*Deus usou a linguagem silenciosa de amor—acoes e nao palavras. Usando os portugueses que estavam na igreja naquele dia, Anna viu atos de bondade, a compaixao, o amor pela familia e comunidade, humildade e reverencia a Deus. Todos o quais, familiar para ela o que parece ser eras atras, ela viu e sentiu como ela olhou em volta dentro da pequena igreja despretensioso.*

*Quando Deus chamou Anna de volta em seus bracos, deus usou o pastor fazer com que o tema seja sobre a graca ou a favor, o name de deus disse a ela que vai ser o nome dela. Deus usou uma linguagem que nao podia falar—Portugues.*

# Author's Message

If you have experienced or is currently experiencing any of Anna's struggles and you are beginning to question God's love for you, stop and question yourself if you have been obeying Him. Anna delayed the fulfillment of God's promise in her life due to her self-imposed disobedience. Once she decided to return and submit to God, she experienced God's permanent provision—health, wealth and happiness. God's way are clever and original including orchestrating events to bring this story to different parts of the world— Australia, Brazil, Canada, China, France, Germany, India, Italy, Mexico, Spain, Philippines, United Kingdom to name a few, even without the author's knowledge, so that others may know that nothing can separate us from God's love.

If the story touched you in anyway, share it with a friend or a loved one.